Walk Your Cat
THE COMPLETE GUIDE

By
Steven Jacobson & Jean Miller

Copyright © Steven Jacobson & Jean Miller, 2008
All rights reserved.

Except where permitted by law, no part of this publication may be reproduced, stored in a retrieval system or transmitted in any form or by any means, including electronic, mechanical, photocopying, recording or otherwise without prior written permission from the authors.

Except as noted below, all artwork © Steven Jacobson & Jean Miller. Artwork on p.29 © Jovan Nikolic | bigstockphoto.com; artwork on p.30 © Marianne Guntow | bigstockphoto.com; artwork on p.103 © Donna Kilday | Dreamstime.com; artwork on p.104 © David Davis | Dreamstime.com; artwork on p.105 © Jkitan | Dreamstime.com.

Note: The authors disclaim any responsibility for any liability, loss, or risk, personal or otherwise, which is incurred as a consequence, directly or indirectly, of the use and application of any of the contents of this book.

Library of Congress Control Number: 2008908480
ISBN 978-0-615-21641-6
Published by Spiraka, Blacksburg, Virginia. Printed in the USA.

Additional copies of this book can be purchased at
www.walkyourcat.com.

SPIRAKA

ACKNOWLEDGMENTS

Our best thanks to Melissa Balmain, Mary Ellen Jones and Mary Cato for their invaluable help and suggestions.

CONTENTS

CHAPTER 1: Introduction..................1
Why Cats Need To Be Walked...2

Can Cats Really Be Walked On A Leash?...5

What Equipment Do You Need?...6

Overview...10

CHAPTER 2: Training Tools..................13
Classical Conditioning...14

Operant Conditioning...15

Guidelines For Training...23

CHAPTER 3: Motivating Your Cat..................26
How To Relate To Your Cat On Its Walks...27

A Natural Motivator...30

The Cat-Walking Principle...32

Breaking The Indoor Routine...33

CHAPTER 4: Where & When to Walk Your Cat........35
Understanding Your Cat's Need For Space...36

Familiarity...38

Activities Outdoors...39

When Is The Best Time To Walk Your Cat?...47

Taking Your Cat To Visit Friends...48

CHAPTER 5: Leash-Training: Part 1 52

Putting Your Cat's Harness On...53

Where To Stand In Relation To Your Cat...56

Handling The Leash...57

Venturing Outdoors...59

Dealing With Conflict...62

CHAPTER 6: Leash-Training: Part 2........................69

Directing Your Cat...70

Controlling Your Cat...78

Vocal Cues...80

Maintenance...84

Walking Two Cats At A Time...86

CHAPTER 7: The Art Of Reassurance......................89

Signs Of Trouble...90

Reassurance Techniques...91

Habituation...94

Desensitization...96

Loss Of Control...98

CHAPTER 8: Learning Catanese............................100

　Your Cat's Body Language...102

CHAPTER 9: Health & Safety...............................109

　Heatstroke...110

　Sunburn...111

　Poisons...112

　Insects...113

　Diseases & Parasites...114

　General Safety Issues...115

CHAPTER 10: Your Cat At A Glance......................118

　Cat Physiology...119

　The Natural Life Of The Modern Domestic Cat...123

REFERENCES...127

INDEX...129

Introduction

CHAPTER 1

Introduction

If indoor cats, as a group, could express themselves by going online and creating their own blogs, what would they talk about? We are willing to bet that the most common topic would be "dealing with boredom." Feline bloggers would write about indoor games and toys, as well as ingenious methods "for getting a human's attention." But the most popular articles would be written by a small group of bloggers—the envy of the online cat community—whose owners take them outdoors for walks! These fortunate bloggers would describe the many wonderful adventures they have had outdoors and offer highly technical discussions over which cat-harnesses are best for walking.

You may be wondering whether your cat is as enthusiastic for going for walks outdoors on a leash as these imaginary tech-savvy felines. In this book, we hope to convince you that it is. In fact, along with showing you how to leash-train your cat and giving you a complete understanding of all aspects of walking cats, we will do our best to convince you that walks on a leash have a natural and important role to play in the life of your cat.

Why Cats Need To Be Walked

At this very minute, there are tens of millions of cats who spend all of their lives indoors, having little or no access to the world outside the confines of their homes. This indoor lifestyle is a relatively new development in the long history of *felis catus*—the domestic cat. It has come about because today many more people live in urban and suburban environments, and also because our attitudes towards our cats have changed.

Perhaps you, like many owners, view your cat as a companion pet or even a member of the family. If so, you are probably quite protective of it, and safety concerns are a primary reason why you keep it indoors. To keep your cat safe, you must lock it securely away from outdoor diseases, traffic and the neighbor's dog. But in doing so, you deny it access to green grass and blue skies, to the thrill of the hunt, and of course, to the social scene of the neighborhood. And you can believe it: your cat knows what it is missing!

Cats have a very real need to go outdoors. This need is often overlooked by owners who feel that there is simply no safe alternative to keeping their cats permanently indoors. Owners may also not fully understand what is it about the outdoors that cats are so drawn to.

> Cats of all ages, temperaments, and breeds will demonstrate a strong desire to go outdoors, if they are given access.
>
> Once your cat gets used to being walked, it will learn to clearly and energetically tell you when it wants to go outside. Your cat may meow, paw at the door, or play with its leash to give you a hint.

What, you may have wondered, is there outdoors that the many creature comforts of indoor living can't make up for? For starters, if you were to put yourself in your cat's boots, you would find that, while you really do appreciate the many benefits of indoor life, your home would be too small and dull to be in *all* of the time. The outdoors is simply so much bigger and more exciting for your cat than any indoor environment could ever be.

Through a window, your cat can only indirectly experience the incomparable variety and intensity of sights, sounds and smells that are found outdoors. And while sense stimulation is very important for cats, your cat's need for the outdoors is fueled by a lot more than just its senses. Cats have natural activities that it is important for them to do—and which can really only be done outdoors. Being unable to pursue these activities combined with a boring indoor environment reduces their quality of life by depriving them of much needed social and behavioral stimulation.

Walk Your Cat

Over time, indoor cats can become bored, depressed, frustrated and less confident. These emotions are often hard to recognize in cats. If your cat appears to be more aloof or withdrawn than you remember, or if it seems grumpy for no apparent reason, it could be suffering from a case of the indoor blues.

> It is especially hard for cats who live in small homes or apartments to get the stimulation they need. These cats are more at risk of becoming depressed, and can especially benefit from being walked.

Buying your cat toys or a companion—while often helpful—can't fully make up for the limitations of indoor life. So if you are considering getting your cat a companion to help with a lack of stimulation, be aware that you might end up with two bored and depressed cats on your hands.

Training your cat to walk on a leash is a far better solution to the problems caused by indoor confinement. When you take your cat for a walk, you *can* be assured that you are providing it with all the stimulation it needs. Even occasional walks will help your cat live a more natural life while still allowing you to keep it safe.

Your cat's physical health will also benefit from the exercise it gets on its walks. But most important, by walking your cat you will be giving it an activity that it truly loves. Even a fifteen minute walk outdoors will be far more rewarding to it than its favorite food treat!

But Can Cats Really Be Walked On A Leash?

Just how well cats respond to leash-training will probably surprise you. Cats are, after all, notorious for being untrainable and many people assume that they won't tolerate being restrained on a leash, much less being controlled on one. But, as you will discover, training your cat to walk on a leash is a lot easier than many other things you may have tried to teach it—staying off the kitchen table, say, or not eating your houseplants. This is because leash-training works with your cat's natural inclinations.

In the following chapters we will introduce you to an approach to training that is based on your cat's natural behaviors. We will help you understand and overcome common pitfalls to successful leash-training. We also take you step by step through a variety of effective techniques that we have learned from years of experience.

How Long Will It Take To Leash-Train Your Cat?

In the course of this book, you will learn to use a variety of behavioral modification techniques to train your cat. These techniques are well known by animal behaviorists and researchers to be very effective in training cats. Since they take time to work, you will need to be patient while training your cat, and trust that the methods you will learn actually work. They really do! You should expect it to take between several weeks and several months of regular walks outdoors before your cat learns to respond fully to its training.

> The behavior modification techniques that we describe are often used successfully to train cats to stop scratching furniture, not to eat house plants, and to eliminate many other behaviors, which cats love but their owners find undesirable.

How quickly *your* cat progresses in its training will also depend on its personality, which is guided by its genes and its history. Your cat's history will be much more important than what breed it is. If your cat is a generally friendly cat that was exposed to many people and animals and handled often as a kitten, it will tend to be more confident outdoors, and take to training faster than cats that were not as well socialized.

What Equipment Do You Need?

When deciding on what equipment to use for walking your cat, think of walks outdoors as mini-hiking trips. Having the right gear will make your walks more pleasant and allow you to focus on training, without having to worry about problems that *will* arise from having the wrong equipment. Here are some suggestions.

Use A Harness—Not A Collar. On its walks, your cat will run, jump, pounce, and dart off, often when you least expect it. It may also pull on its leash vigorously—even to the point of

Introduction 7

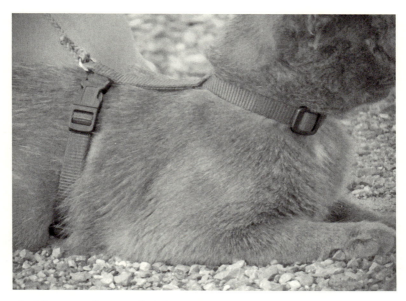

choking—as it eagerly tries to reach something that has caught its interest. A harness, which has a torso strap in addition to a neck strap, helps reduce pressure on your cat's neck when it pulls against the leash. But be aware that some harnesses are better than others. Avoid ones that have the leash attached directly to the neck strap. They are no better than collars in protecting your cat's neck.

Make sure the straps on the harness cannot tighten on your cat's neck or torso when the leash is pulled! You can, in fact, buy harnesses like this and if you use them you risk strangling your cat. Additionally, your cat will react violently in an attempt to free itself from something tightening around its neck or body, and you will find it hard to loosen the straps with your cat in a panic.

Avoid impractical harnesses. Some harnesses are designed more for cat owners than for cats. Avoid harnesses that are made primarily of string. They are inexpensive, but are not suitable for walking cats. Likewise, avoid harnesses that are *too* heavy, restrictive, or bulky so that they interfere with your cat's outdoor activities. Also, keep in mind that cats actually feel with their fur, and your cat will not want to be covered up.

We recommend using an H-style cat harness as shown on the previous page. These are ideal for directing your cat. They are also, in our experience, the simplest harnesses to put on and take off a cat. When choosing a harness, ease of putting the harness on your cat should be one of your foremost considerations.

The harness should use side-release buckles, which lock shut on top of your cat's back rather than underneath it. A harness that is not easy to put on will become a great liability to your cat's training. Side-release buckles make putting on and taking off the harness a breeze, especially if you can avoid reaching under your cat to do so. Having the buckles located on top of your cat's back also allows you to keep your hands out of the way of your cat's defenses, namely, its teeth and claws.

For a leash, use a 1/8 inch, ten foot brightly-colored nylon or polyethylene cord. A ten foot leash is suitable for all the activities you will allow your cat to do outdoors but short enough to maintain control. It is a good idea to use a brightly-colored or even fluorescent leash as this helps prevent you or anyone else from tripping over the leash. You

Introduction

can buy a small roll of this cord in many retail stores that have a sporting section.

The leash should be securely, and permanently, *tied to the harness.* Often, pet leashes use lanyard or snap hooks, but there are reasons not to use them when walking cats. Hooks would be useful if you wanted to detach the leash from the harness and let your cat run free in its harness. However, you should never do this, as harnesses do not have safety release features like cat collars do to protect your cat if it gets snagged on something. If you do decide to use a lanyard or snap hook be aware that the smaller hooks often sold with cat leashes, even metal ones, can weaken and break with repeated use.

Tie a handle on the leash yourself rather than using a weighted handle. Cats are sensitive to sudden loud noises and should you accidentally drop the leash, the noise a weighted handle would make could cause your cat to run away in a panic. (We speak from experience.) A hand-made grip, as shown below, can be held securely and be quickly removed if your cat manages to get itself into a bind and you need to untangle the leash.

PUTTING THE HARNESS ON—A WORD OF CAUTION

When you put the harness on or take it off your cat, pay careful attention to which strap goes on, or off, first. *Always attach the harness to the neck first, and only then around the torso.* The reason is that when you are putting the harness on, your cat may try to run away from you and could escape. The danger is that if the harness is attached only to the torso and your cat escapes, the harness can tie your cat's back legs when it runs and could injure it. Securing the neck strap first also allows you to better control your cat.

Similarly, the harness should always be taken off in the reverse order. *Undo the harness from the torso first and then from around the neck.*

A useful tip for putting the harness collar around your cat's neck is to keep your hands (and the collar) close to its neck under the chin. This prevents you from blocking your cat's vision, which is sure to annoy it, and also keeps your hands out of reach of its claws and teeth.

Overview Of This Book

Training your cat to walk on a leash involves a lot more than what you might normally think of as 'leash-training.' This is

Introduction

why this book is called "Walk Your Cat" and not "Leash-Train Your Cat." In the following chapters, you will learn everything you need to train your cat to walk on a leash. You will also learn how the training techniques we show you work. All cats are different and we hope that by understanding the reasons behind these techniques, you can adapt them more easily, if needed, to your cat's own unique personality and abilities.

In the next chapter, Training Tools, we describe the basic training principles you will need to train your cat to walk on a leash.

The methods you will learn in Training Tools only work if you can properly motivate your cat. Being able to motivate your cat effectively will make all the difference between its walks being a drag or being as graceful as a ballet. In chapter 3, Motivating Your Cat, you will learn how to properly motivate your cat to cooperate with you while on a leash.

Chapter 4, Where & When To Walk Your Cat & What To Do When You Get There, describes all the activities your cat will want to do when you take it outdoors.

Chapter 5, Leash-Training: Part 1, explains how to handle your cat on a leash and describes techniques for eliminating the most common types of conflict that arise when walking a cat on a leash.

Chapter 6, Leash-Training: Part 2, builds upon previous chapters to show you how to control and direct your cat using a combination of leash and vocal cues.

For your cat's walks to be smooth and relaxed, you will need to be able to recognize when your cat is nervous, and then be able to reassure it. Chapters 7 and 8, The Art Of Reassurance and Learning Catanese, help you to deal with your cat's cautious nature while outdoors. You will find these chapters especially useful if your cat tends to be shy or timid.

12 Walk Your Cat

In chapter 9, Health & Safety, you will learn about common dangers outdoors and how to protect your cat while on a walk.

Last, but not least, in chapter 10, Your Cat At A Glance, we provide additional information about cats and their behavior that we think you will find useful when training and walking your cat.

You will benefit most from this book if you read it in its entirety *before* you begin training your cat. This will allow you to avoid experiencing first hand common, but easily avoidable, pitfalls that lie in wait for you and your cat along the path to successful leash-training. You can refer back to relevant sections as needed in the course of your cat's training.

We believe that by the time you finish reading this book, you'll agree that walks outdoors on a leash have a natural and important role to play in the life of your, and *all,* indoor cats. Walking your cat, even occasionally, can truly change its life for the better and strengthen your bond with it. So our advice to you before you embark on training is to remember that walking your cat is primarily for *its* benefit. Go at your cat's pace and don't forget, wherever possible, to allow it to stop and smell the roses.

CHAPTER 2

Training Tools

Did you know that some cats, when hunting a mouse that has hidden itself in the grass, may tap the ground with their paws in order to spook the mouse into running and thereby revealing itself? You have probably witnessed your cat doing equally clever things. Cats are not born with a bag of tricks for hunting. Instead, they readily learn these and many other clever behaviors using the methods you will learn about in this chapter.

You will take advantage of these methods, which cats naturally use to learn, to train your cat to walk on a leash. The training methods in this chapter are not unique to leash-training cats (or to cats for that matter), and you will also find them useful if you want to train your cat in other ways.

Classical Conditioning

The most identifiable way that cats learn is through what is known as *classical conditioning*. You have probably witnessed this type of learning in your cat. Does your cat come running whenever it hears you opening a can of food? If so, its excitement is an automatic response that your cat developed when it first associated the presence of its dinner with the sound of a can being opened.

Your cat only needed to hear the sound of a can being opened once or twice for it to make the connection between the sound and its food. The ability to make quick connections like this is invaluable to cats in the wild who use indirect cues, such as the sound of grass rustling, to recognize the presence of prey or danger.

Cats can be trained using classical conditioning by teaching them to associate an indirect cue with something that they really want. Food is an obvious thing that cats really want, but as you will see in following chapters, there are other things that your cat will find even more compelling than food.

Classical conditioning is useful for cats, but it does have a downside. Your cat may mistakenly associate a frightening incident with something or someone who is present but is not really connected to the incident. For instance, if your cat is scared by a sudden loud noise just as you are introducing it to someone, it may instantly develop a fear of that person. Fortunately, your cat has the ability to learn that it has made a mistake, and it has no reason to fear that person, as you will discover in the section *Desensitization* in Chapter 5.

> More than a century ago, Russian scientist Ivan Pavlov famously demonstrated learning through classical conditioning by showing that he could get his dogs to drool whenever they heard a bell ringing. He did this by teaching them to associate the sound of a bell with the presence of food.

Operant Conditioning

The type of learning you will take advantage of most when training your cat is called *operant conditioning*. In this type of learning, your cat changes the way it behaves to get something it wants or to avoid something it dislikes. Your cat pays attention to the results of its actions and if it likes the outcome of something it does, it will be inclined to repeat that behavior. If it doesn't like the outcome, it will learn to avoid doing it.

Your cat learns to meow in specific ways around you because it likes how you respond to these sounds—you give it the attention it is seeking. Cats are ingenious at getting their owner's attention using nonvocal means too. Your cat uses its body posture, facial expressions, and specific behaviors to evoke responses from you that it wants. These are skills it has also learned using operant conditioning.

By controlling the outcome of your cat's actions, you can use operant conditioning to change the way it behaves. Operant conditioning can, for instance, be used to get your cat to respond to your directing it on a leash, or to make it stop howling at the door at night in an attempt to get you to take it outdoors.

Rewards And Punishments

You train your cat using operant conditioning by giving it incentives—rewards and punishments—to do what you want. What will work as a reward for your cat depends on its preferences, but generally food treats, petting, sweet talking, and, of course, going for a walk are all effective rewards.

Whenever your cat behaves in a way that you like, give it a reward. After being rewarded many times, your cat will make a connection between the behavior and the reward. It will then repeat the behavior *hoping* that it will get a reward.

> Because training using operant conditioning involves having your cat understand the connection between a reward (or punishment) and a behavior, while you are still training your cat you should reward (or punish) it *every time* it repeats the behavior to help it most quickly make the connection.

Training Tools

Some examples of punishments that are commonly recommended for training cats are: yelling at the cat, or making a loud noise near it; spraying it with water; or taking something that it likes away from it. The last example is the *only* punishment that you should use when leash-training your cat.

Punishments play a very small role in training your cat to walk on a leash. There are two reasons for this. The first is that you are mainly trying to create new behaviors in your cat and punishments are only appropriate if you want to get your cat to stop doing things. The second reason is that, even for eliminating behaviors, in most situations, training cats with punishments is fraught with difficulties.

If you punish your cat to stop it from doing something, it is more likely to associate the punishment with you than with the behavior you are trying to eliminate. From its point of view, you are the cause of the unpleasantness it has just experienced, not the activity it was busy enjoying when you punished it. The lesson your cat will learn from being punished is to be wary of you, or that it should avoid you. For walking your cat, this would obviously be problematic.

Indirect punishments, such as spraying your cat with water using a spray bottle, are sometimes recommended for training cats because they can *temporarily* fool your cat into associating a punishment with a behavior you are punishing it for. The difference between a direct and an indirect punishment is that your cat cannot identify the source of the punishment. But indirect punishments, too, will eventually fail as your cat will learn to associate your presence with the punishment. In the above example, it will learn that you are the one spraying it.

Another difficulty with using punishments is that it is hard to find the right level of punishment to use. Too weak a punishment will yield only scorn from your cat, and too severe a punishment will cause your cat to be afraid of you.

While punishments can be effective in some circumstances, it is generally best to avoid them given the problems using them. Fortunately, there are more effective ways to encourage or discourage behaviors in your cat. Two such methods are *Futility* and *Replacement*.

> Punishments are useful sometimes. If your cat tries to sneak out the door whenever you come in or go out, try shaking a can or bottle with stones in it to make a loud noise, which your cat will want to avoid.

Futility (Extinction)

Training using futility (often called extinction) works as follows. Let's say you want to stop your cat from howling at the door in the middle of the night in an attempt to get you to take it out (regrettably, this is not a made up example). Instead of repeatedly removing your cat from the door or punishing it, you simply resist its pleas and completely ignore it. After a while, your cat will learn that howling is a waste of its energy and it will gradually stop doing it.

But be aware that this approach will first lead your cat to increase both the amount and volume of its howling as it tries harder to get your attention before finally giving up. For training using futility to work, you must *never* give your cat any reason to think that its behavior, in this case howling, will get it what it wants. If you even occasionally show that you are paying attention to your cat, or worse, give it what it wants, it will be difficult to eliminate the behavior.

Replacement

Replacement is an approach in which you replace unwanted behaviors in your cat with ones that you find more acceptable. For instance, to stop your cat from scratching furniture, you can encourage it to use a substitute scratch-post. Another useful application of this approach is for stopping your cat from jumping on the dinner table. If this is a problem you have with your cat, try giving it an alternative place that is higher than the table to perch on. This works because, as you probably know, cats love high places. In this example, it is worth remembering that your cat may be jumping on the table because of a conditioned response to food it has previously received there. So you will also need to detrain this behavior by never feeding your cat on the table.

The Importance Of Timing

When you reward or punish your cat, you must take care that your cat understands exactly which behavior it is being rewarded or punished for. If you wait too long after your cat has done something you consider good before you reward it, it won't be able to make the association between the behavior and the reward. Instead, it might associate the reward with another behavior you had not intended to encourage. The same is true for punishing your cat for undesirable behaviors. A reward or punishment should be given within seconds and no longer than half a minute from when the behavior occurred. If possible, it should be given *while your cat is still engaged in the behavior.*

THE STREETWISE CAT

Earlier we used the example of a cat tapping the ground with its paw to try and locate a mouse hidden in the grass. How does it learn this clever trick? This behavior was learned using operant conditioning. The cat first notices that when it makes a noise (the behavior), the mouse moves and also makes a noise (the reward). The cat then learns to purposely make a noise by tapping the ground.

This example also shows the excellent problem-solving skills for which cats are known. One reason why cats are good at solving problems is the fact that they energetically search for solutions using a trial and error approach. On walks with your cat, you are likely to see this at work, whether it be your cat showing its cunning when hunting a mouse or being quite clever in trying to outsmart you in order to get its own way.

Cats also learn by observing and mimicking the behaviors of other cats. This method of learning is especially important for kittens who learn from their mothers and other family members by copying what they do. People with multiple cats often see this type of learning when one of their cats adopts a behavior previously only seen in another. For instance, one cat learns to use a cat-door by watching another using it.

Bridge Words

If a reward or punishment cannot be given to your cat quickly enough after it does the behavior you are training, you can use a *bridge word* to help it understand why it is being rewarded or punished. A bridge word, as the name suggests, is a designated word that you teach your cat to help it connect a behavior you are training with a particular reward or punishment.

As an example of using bridge words, let's say that, for some reason, you want to encourage your cat to jump onto a particular chair in your house. Each time it jumps on that chair you will reward it by giving it a food treat. If you are unable to give your cat the treat quickly enough after seeing it jump on the chair, you can instead let it know that a treat is forthcoming by repeatedly saying, "Treat" until you can give it one. In this way, your cat will associate a reward with it jumping up on that particular chair even though it was not given a treat immediately after having done so.

It is easy to understand why bridge words work. In fact, you have probably already seen your cat associate a sound with a reward. Think of the earlier example of a cat that comes running when it hears the sound of a can being opened. You could just as easily make the cat associate the presence of food with a word as with the sound of the can being opened. The word 'breakfast,' for instance, can be used to cue the cat that it will soon be fed.

Shaping

Using rewards, you can teach your cat new behaviors that build upon behaviors you have previously taught it. This is commonly known as *shaping*. Your cat, in effect, will grow mentally as you teach it complex behaviors, which it learns in a series of steps. In the chapter, Leash-Training: Part 2, you will use shaping to train your cat to respond to your directing it.

Maintenance

Training a cat is, in one respect, like buying a car or a house. Once you have done it, you will need to maintain it. Cats have a tendency to forget trained behaviors unless they are given occasional reminders of the connection between the behaviors and the rewards used initially to train them.

If you were to completely stop rewarding your cat for a behavior once it has learned it, it will see no need to do the behavior and will stop doing it. But provided you occasionally reward your cat after it does the behavior, it will continue to do it motivated *just by the possibility* of getting a reward.

So what does 'occasionally' mean? Try reducing how often you reward your cat and see if it continues to do the behavior. And if your cat stops doing the behavior, reward it more often.

It is important that your cat is not able to predict when it will get a reward. Therefore, it is best to give rewards randomly rather than, say, every fifth time your cat does the behavior. Maintenance is particularly simple for leash-training and walking your cat, as you will see in the next chapter.

Guidelines For Training

By using operant conditioning, and as much as possible using rewards rather than punishments, you will be most effective when training your cat. Below we suggest two other things you can do to make your cat more receptive to its training. Both involve helping your cat understand what it is you want it to do. If your cat is not responding to its training, it is a fair bet that the problem is that *you* are not communicating properly with it.

Stay On Message

For your cat to clearly understand what you are telling it, you must be consistent in the messages you send it. Establishing good habits when training your cat is the way to do this. Consider, for example, trying to teach your cat to stop jumping on the dinner table by using futility. Whenever your cat jumps on the table, you quickly put it back on the floor. Doing this *every time* your cat jumps on the table will teach your cat that it is futile to jump on the table and it will gradually stop doing it. But if you occasionally let it stay on the table, it will continue to jump up *because of the possibility* that it will be allowed to stay on the table.

It can often be difficult to be consistent and resist your cat's heart-tugging (or nagging) and those large beseeching eyes. But when training your cat, it is important not to be swayed by your cat's attempts to get its own way. In the long run, sticking to your guns and saying, "No" is well worth it. As you learn the techniques and tips in this book, treat them as rules that should *always* be followed. Make them a routine part of your cat's walks. Cats are creatures of habit and, over time, your cat will get used to them.

Understand That Your Cat's Perspective Is Different From Yours

When you communicate with your cat, you should be aware that, even if it responds as you hoped, your cat might not have understood what you communicated in the way you intended. Consider the previous example of training your cat not to jump on the dinner table. Whenever it jumps up, you immediately take it off and put it back on the floor. How will your cat understand this? Will it think to itself: "My owner is trying to tell me that being on the table is bad. I trust my owner so I'll stop doing it"? No. The fact is that your cat is seeing this interaction with you from an entirely feline point of view.

Cats instinctively like high places. And your cat, too, will always think high places are a good thing. Repeatedly taking it off the table won't change its preferences. Your cat will, in fact, not be able to understand why you don't want it on the table. And this is why its training will not work as you intended.

The problem with continually taking it off the table is that your cat will only draw the conclusion that it shouldn't jump on the table *when you are present*. When you are not around, it will continue to jump on the table. Cats can be annoyingly logical! But, by realizing that cats have a preference for high places, you might try giving it an alternative "high place" to jump on. This is a more effective approach than repeatedly taking it off the table.

Training Tools

Understanding your cat's perspective will go a long way toward helping you train it. In chapter 10, we provide information that will help you understand your cat a little better and how it sees the world around it.

26   Walk Your Cat

CHAPTER 3

Motivating Your Cat

The training methods described in the last chapter rely on your being able to provide your cat with suitable rewards or punishments to motivate it to change its behavior. Without them, you will not be able to train your cat, no matter how smart it is. When training most animals, including cats, motivation is a more important factor for success than intelligence.

As you read in the last chapter, cats have no problem learning and can be quite clever. However, it is generally quite difficult to motivate them, which explains why they are difficult to train. Fortunately, when it comes to leash-training, it is easy to find compelling rewards and punishments to motivate them. As a result, leash-training your cat is a relatively easy thing to do. One aspect, though, that might make leash-training your cat difficult for you is the unintuitive role you will have to play when you walk it.

How To Relate To Your Cat On Its Walks

The difficulty in motivating cats stems from the fact that, as a species, they are very independent and self-reliant animals. They can feed and fend for themselves and, other than for socializing, do not have to rely on other cats. This self-reliance makes them their own bosses who answer to no one but themselves.

> Cats simply don't relate to the concept of leaders and followers. Within any group of cats living together, you will not find any one cat that is treated as a leader by the others. This stands in strong contrast to human societies, which are largely hierarchical with groups of people often divided into leaders and followers, bosses and subordinates. This difference in social behavior between humans and cats can cause confusion for cat owners when it comes to training their cats and even just interacting with them in general.

Because of this, the first thing to say about how you should relate to your cat on its walks is that the way *not* to relate to it is as a Drill Sergeant or an Olympic coach. Your cat does not see you as a boss or a leader and it won't do what you want simply to get your approval.

It is not uncommon for owners to believe that they can compel their cats to do what they want—if only they could get them to understand what it is they want them to do. But the reality is that following orders is just not something that it is natural for cats to do. Bossing your cat around will not motivate it to cooperate but *will* instead slow or halt its training.

So if your cat doesn't see you as a boss, how does it view you? And how should you relate to it on walks? The way to relate to your cat is as a parent—or more precisely, a feline parent. And since kittens are always raised by their mothers, your cat views you, if not as its mother then as a maternal figure.

Why would your cat see you as a parental figure? You care for your cat, feed it, play with it and generally treat it in a way that is recognizable to it as the way that a mother cat treats her kittens. As a result, your cat exists, in many ways, in a prolonged state of kittenhood. And this ensures a mother cat-kitten type relationship between you and your cat.

So when training and walking your cat, think of yourself as your cat's guide, or perhaps as a chaperone. If you do this, it will see your presence on its walks in a positive light and will be more accepting of you controlling it on a leash.

We should add that while your cat doesn't need you to go outside for a walk and would almost certainly prefer to go out on its own, it will take advantage of your presence whenever it feels nervous or afraid. It will readily accept and even expect guidance and reassurance from you, much as a kitten receives

DIGGING DEEPER—CAT VS DOG

Why are dogs easier to train than cats? While cats are independent animals and will generally not respond to punishment or disapproval from their owners, dogs will. This is because dogs are pack animals and naturally live in groups that are rigidly hierarchical, led by a dominant alpha animal—usually an intact male. Dogs transfer their pack behavior to their life among humans, with their owners taking on the role of the alpha animal. A dog's owner's approval is in itself a reward for a dog, and this makes dogs trainable in ways that cats can't be.

Cats do not view their owners as authority figures. This is evident from the fact that cats don't display the submissive body postures that dogs do. When a dog lies on its back, it may be saying, "I accept that you are the boss". But when a cat does this, it is saying "come closer, I want to play."

Cats that are strongly bonded to their owners will respond to some degree to their owner's disapproval. However, this leverage isn't sufficient to train them.

from its mother. You can help your cat confront and become used to new things it encounters during a walk. You can also help it learn to trust things that in the past have frightened it. In short, it will trust your judgment and draw confidence from you to boldly go where it has not gone before.

A Natural Motivator

The discussion in the last section may still leave you wondering how you can get your cat to cooperate with you. Without the innate sense of obedience that dogs have, how can you

really expect any success in leash-training your cat? What reason does your cat have to change the way it behaves and to tolerate you controlling it on a leash?

The answer is that your cat has a strong natural motivation to go for walks on a leash. Unlike teaching your cat to do tricks, like shaking hands or rolling over, going for walks is a reward in itself for your cat and doesn't require any additional motivation.

We should clarify that your cat will not be motivated for you to walk it around *indoors*. It is actually the access to the outdoors that motivates it. To understand this a little better, let's briefly delve behind those large quizzical eyes for a better understanding of what your cat finds so appealing outdoors.

Why Your Cat Needs Access To The Outdoors

When your cat sits on the window sill and looks out so earnestly, it sees the world in the context of what can be called its *natural life*. The natural life is the life your cat would lead if it lived independently of you and other human beings, living and surviving on its wits and instincts.

Living free and on its own, your cat would do all those activities that cats in the wild do. It would seek out and make a home in an area that would provide it with food, shelter, security and social contact with other cats. You can read more about the natural life in chapter 10.

Your cat is built physically and mentally for this life. Domestication, and indoor life, have changed your cat's nature very little, and it has not lost its drive to pursue these natural activities. Your cat, for instance, retains its drive and abilities to hunt despite being well fed and having no real need to hunt. And while your cat can, to a limited extent, do some of its natural activities indoors, most can only be fully realized outdoors. This, along with the incomparable level of stimulation found outdoors, makes going outdoors extremely appealing to your cat.

The Cat-Walking Principle

Your cat's desire to go outdoors and to act out its natural life gives you all the leverage you need to train it to be walked on a leash. No additional rewards are needed! *Your cat's desire to go outdoors far outweighs its reluctance to be restrained in a harness and be controlled by you.* This is the most important principle to remember when training your cat. A caveat to this principle is that if you handle your cat incorrectly you can lose all of the leverage over it that you have gained by taking it outdoors. Incorrect handling will cause conflict between you and your cat and make it uncooperative.

How do you take advantage of this principle to train your cat? First of all, you must ensure that your cat gets the most out of its walks. You can do this by allowing it plenty of opportunities to do all of its natural activities. In the next chapter, we discuss all the things your cat will want to do when you take it outdoors. Allowing it to do them will keep its motivation high and make it a willing participant in its training.

As for handling your cat correctly, you want to make sure that your cat doesn't object to your presence when you are walking it. We have already said that if you try to dominate your cat, it will react negatively. Additionally, for your cat to be comfortable with your presence, it must know that you will not force it into situations it feels are threatening and also that you will not interfere too much with it doing things outdoors that it enjoys.

More generally, your presence should not stress your cat out in any way. Cats become stressed when they are restrained, forced into a situation unwillingly, punished, handled unpredictably or are physically uncomfortable.

> Your cat's mood can let you know if it is experiencing physical discomfort. You can read about signs of physical discomfort and how to protect your cat's health outdoors in chapter 9, Health & Safety.

You might expect that when leash-training your cat, it can be difficult to avoid conflict arising. After all, training involves restraining your cat and taking it to places it may not want to go. Fortunately, it is not hard to avoid conflict between you and your cat as you will see in the chapter Leash-Training: Part 1.

Breaking The Indoor Routine

If your cat has not had any recent exposure to the outdoors, it may initially not show interest in going outside when you first open the door to let it out. This is not due to a lack of interest in going out, but is because it has become set in its indoor routine. Your cat will need some time to adjust to the new possibility that it can go outdoors.

You can help your cat adjust more quickly by repeatedly picking it up and taking it outside, allowing it to look around for a few minutes. This will get it thinking about the all the adventures that await it out there. If you are concerned about taking your cat outdoors without a leash and harness, you can instead hold the door slightly ajar (though not wide enough for it to escape) and wait for it to show interest in what's on the other side of the door. With either of these methods, your cat will soon understand that the outdoors has become accessible to it.

One point to note is that you must make sure there is nothing that will scare your cat in the vicinity of the door. If there is something that your cat will have to pass by that makes it nervous, you should, if possible, take another route. But if there is no alternative route, you will need to take the time to accustom your cat to whatever is frightening it. In chapter 7, The Art Of Reassurance, we show you how to do this.

Where & When... **35**

Where & When To Walk Your Cat & What To Do When You Get There

The most noticeable difference between walking cats and walking dogs is the importance of picking the right places to take them. Cats have special requirements when it comes to the places they go, which ensure that they are able to keep themselves safe from the variety of creatures they might encounter. So, when deciding where to walk your cat, you should look for places where it will feel safe. And since you want your cat to enjoy its walks, you will also want to pick places that it will find stimulating.

Understanding Your Cat's Need For Space

For any cat, feeling safe in the presence of other animals means always being able to keep at a comfortable distance from them. In fact, keeping out of one another's space is a normal part of the social behavior of cats.

Your cat, on its own, would not walk in places where it would have no choice but to get too close to any animal that it doesn't personally know and that might be a threat to it. And in particular, your cat will be very cautious around animals from species it does not recognize. Should your cat come across an unfamiliar animal, it might run away from it, even if the animal is relatively far away. Not knowing anything about that animal, your cat won't know if it is a threat or how easy it would be to escape from it should it attack.

Your cat will likely recognize most of the creatures it will come across on a walk and know whether it should be concerned about them or not. Your cat probably regards humans, and other cats, for instance, as being generally harmless. Nonetheless, when your cat encounters another cat or a human it does not personally know, it will probably want to keep at a safe distance from them until it has gotten to know, and trust them.

> As a general rule, expect that your cat will want to keep at least six feet between it and any animal it doesn't personally know.

Location, Location, Location

Is there a best place to walk? Yes, the ideal place, which is also the most obvious, is a back or front yard directly accessible from your home. This is a very natural arrangement for your cat, as you can read about in the section The Natural Life Of The Modern Domestic Cat, in chapter 10. If you do not have a yard, consider walking your cat in a quiet neighborhood, a public park, or a friend's yard. Wherever you take your cat, make sure that you are able to keep it safe and also that it feels comfortable walking there.

> Since you are restraining your cat on a leash, it is less able to protect itself from danger. Therefore, your cat's safety is your responsibility. Even if your cat felt comfortable doing it, you should not walk your cat in places where you would not be able to keep it safe. Avoid heavy traffic of any kind, and places where dogs or other animals are allowed to run free.

Based on what we said above, a good example of a place that is *not* suitable to walk your cat is a busy sidewalk. But places that aren't crowded may also be a problem if your cat will encounter any creatures there that it doesn't recognize.

When you think of the phrase "creatures your cat doesn't recognize," you probably think of 'wildebeest,' 'giant octopus' or similar exotic animals. But for your cat it refers to any unknown thing that can move or make noise. So the list of things that your cat will be wary of does not only include the animals listed above, but also cars, cyclists and clowns for example, as your cat may not have encountered them before either. Consequently, zoos, bike paths and sci-fi conventions are probably not good choices for walking your cat.

Familiarity

It can take weeks or months for your cat to feel completely safe walking in a new location. As your cat becomes comfortable on its walks, it will develop an attachment to the area. It will create a mental map of its surroundings, identifying escape routes and places to hide and climb, figuring out how to get from one place to another and also remembering where it has previously located potential prey. It will be especially interested in returning to those places.

The familiarity your cat has with its surroundings will have a noticeable impact on its walks. If your cat feels safe, walks will be smooth and relaxed, but if it is nervous, walks will be slow and erratic. This is one reason why it is a good idea to walk your cat repeatedly in the same locations.

Does this mean you should restrict your walks to the same area and not walk it anywhere else? No. Cats are as curious as they are cautious. Once your cat learns to feel safe in a place, it will become emboldened to do some exploring and you can slowly expand the size of the area you walk it in.

Additionally, your cat will undoubtably appreciate you adding a little variety to its walks. Being taken to new places every once in a while, such as a trip to a park or to a friend's yard, can be very stimulating and enjoyable for it.

> When your cat gets scared—for whatever reason—it will likely turn on its heels and make a beeline for home. Therefore, when walking your cat in a new place, it is especially important to have complete control of it. Having your cat get loose in a place it is unfamiliar with can be a disaster.

Activities Outdoors

In the preceding sections, we have provided general guidelines to use when deciding where you will walk your cat. There is one more factor you should consider when choosing a location, which brings us back to the reason for walking your cat in the first place. Taking your cat for walks provides it with access to the outdoors and the opportunity to do activities it cannot do indoors. And in this respect, not all places outdoors will be equally interesting to your cat.

Your cat is strongly motivated to pursue its natural activities, as we discussed in The Cat Walking Principle in the last chapter. But can walking your cat on a leash really allow it to pursue these activities? You may be surprised to learn that while

40   Walk Your Cat

on a leash, your cat can do most, if not all, of the things it would do if it were allowed out on its own.

Scent Messaging

So, what will your cat want to do when you take it outdoors? To begin with, it will want to explore, taking time to stop and smell grass blades, plants, bushes and other objects in order to inspect scent marks left by other cats, neighborhood pets and wildlife. These scent marks are imperceptible to humans, but cats' noses are designed to easily detect them. This is how cats keep tabs on their *territory* and *home range*. You can read about the importance of territory and home range to your cat in chapter 10. As your cat walks from place to place, it learns which animals are there or have recently passed by. It will seek out and

Where & When...

readily find the scent marks left by cats and other animals. Your cat will be especially on alert for the scent of potential prey.

Your cat, too, will want to leave its scent by leaving glandular secretions on objects it rubs up against during its walks. All this scent marking by your cat and others in the area is very important to them. Felines, both wild and domestic, use scent marks to communicate. Scent marking allows cats to communicate without having to get close to each other and risk a confrontation. Because scent marks erode over time, your cat will want to go outdoors frequently to refresh its marks. Taking your cat out often allows it to remain current on the state of its home range.

> In many ways, communicating with scent marks is similar to communicating with e-mail. With a distinctive eagerness, indoor cats on a daily basis want to go out and check for messages left by other animals. And like with e-mail, once outdoors, cats send and receive messages without actually coming into physical contact with any other animal. Correspondents do not even need to be present at the same time to carry on a conversation.

Scratching

Cats will also leave scent marks when they scratch objects with their claws. This is because they have scent glands between their toes. However, when your cat scratches something, it is *not* doing so to leave messages for other cats to find. Cats tend to ignore each other's scratch marks. Cats scratch because it helps them shed the outermost sheath of their claws and gives their muscles a good stretch as they do so. It may also provide them with self-assurance. If you walk by a log or other piece of wood on the ground, your cat will often want to stop and scratch it. It may even develop a favorite scratching spot.

Grazing

Walks outdoors give your cat much-needed exercise, which will help keep it healthy and trim. Cats generally need more physical activity than they can get indoors and it is not surprising that obesity is a common problem for indoor cats.

There are also other health benefits to taking your cat outdoors. Eating grass or other plants—often unavailable indoors—is beneficial for cats. It helps them cough up hair swallowed during grooming. Additionally, many cats enjoy

Where & When...

wild catnip, which is found throughout most of the US. It has the same effect on them as commercially sold catnip. Eating greenery is often the first thing cats do when let outside. But stopping to graze like little cows will only occupy them for a short while.

Tree Climbing

At times, for no apparent reason, your cat will break into a run. Perhaps it just wants to stretch its legs. But often these bursts of speed will be directed at a nearby tree. Tree climbing is an important survival skill for cats. It is their prefered method of escape from danger. Being up a tree also provides a good vantage point from which cats can look over their territory and home range. Climbing in itself is pleasurable for cats as it is a good way for them to stretch their shoulder and back muscles.

However, if you let your cat climb trees, beware! If your cat manages to get too high up into the branches of a tree, you may have to climb up and carry it down, or worse you may be unable to get it down. But you can let your cat climb trees without any problems so long as you use caution and common sense.

If your cat climbs a tree, make sure that it remains on the trunk or on a low and easy to reach branch. Also take care that you do not let go of the leash as your cat begins its ascent. To allow your cat to climb a tree safely, give it sufficient leash to start climbing the tree trunk, then provide enough resistance to prevent it from climbing higher than you want it to. But be careful not to pull your cat off the tree. We discuss additional safety issues for letting your cat climb while on a leash in chapter 9: Health & Safety.

To get down from the tree, your cat will back down on its own. Cats' curved claws prevent them from climbing head-first down a tree so when your cat descends it may seem like it is struggling. If you choose, you can help your cat down by plucking it off the tree and placing it on the ground, but your cat will likely be annoyed by your interference.

Hunting

Of all the outdoor activities that cats can do on a leash, the one that might surprise you the most is hunting. Cats can, in fact, be quite successful hunters while on a leash. They naturally prefer to hunt at short distances rather than engaging in long chases, which their bodies are not designed for. A ten foot leash provides your cat ample room for hunting rodents, insects or other small prey.

If you do allow your cat to hunt, be prepared to make a decision about what to do if it catches anything. While domestic cats usually do not eat prey that they catch, it is generally not a good idea to let your cat consume rodents or other animals it catches. See our chapter on Health & Safety for potential dangers of letting your cat eat prey. If you do not want your cat to hunt (which is probably a good idea if you are squeamish), you can still allow it to stalk prey and simply prevent it from catching anything. This is better than not letting it hunt at all.

Resting

An easy to overlook activity that your cat will want to do outdoors is resting. Simply sitting in the fresh air for a while is more than just a break from other activities for your cat. So when your cat does sit or lie down, remember that it *is* doing one of its favorite activities.

Your cat will be thrilled at the opportunity to go out to roam, to scratch its claws, to scent mark, to climb and to hunt. But along with these activities, just being outside is pleasurable for your cat. Rolling in the dirt, sitting in the fresh air, basking in the warm sunlight or resting in the shade for a short while will all be a great source of enjoyment for it.

When Is The Best Time To Walk Your Cat?

You and your cat may not agree on this. If it were up to your cat, the most desirable times to go out are when the light is most favorable for hunting. These are dawn, dusk and noon. As cats have excellent night vision, your cat may express an interest in going out when it is dark. It's best not to give in since your own night vision probably isn't good enough for you to control and protect your cat outdoors at night.

For your part, perhaps like many people, finding time in a busy schedule to walk your cat can be a challenge. But so long as the weather is not too hot or too cold, or too wet, your cat will usually be quite happy to go out whenever it suits you.

> Surprisingly, cats don't mind walking in light rain or snow. When walking in bad weather though, let your cat decide when it has had enough and always allow it to go back indoors when it wants.

Taking Your Cat To Visit Friends

Teaching your cat to walk on a leash creates a new opportunity for your cat to socialize with other cats. If you have a friend who owns an indoor cat that has also been trained to walk on a leash, you can consider letting them get to know each other. Aside from being a fun social activity for you, why would you want to do this?

Cats are generally considered to be asocial. However, while the way that cats socialize with each other is very different, and seemingly strange, to the way humans socialize, domestic cats nonetheless still benefit from the presence of other cats, which are a source of positive stimulation for them. Additionally, having your cat become accustomed to your friends and their cats will help it become more comfortable around people and cats in general.

> Domestic cats, because of their association with humans, are more sociable animals than their wilder counterparts. As a result, the label 'asocial' often does not fit very well with house cats.

How will your cat react to the presence of another cat? If you have ever tried to introduce a new cat into your home or had a stray cat come sit outside your window, your cat most likely became uncharacteristically aggressive towards the other cat. This might lead you to believe that your cat is anti-social. But there is a perfectly logical explanation for your cat's behavior.

Where & When... **49**

Cats are territorial, meaning that they will protect the area they consider their territory from intrusion by strange cats. So your cat's aggressive reaction to the strange cat was your cat trying to protect its territory from an intruder. For free-roaming and indoor-outdoor cats, this space includes a large area around their primary home. But for indoor cats, their territory is limited to the inside of the homes where they live.

When you take your cat outdoors, it does not consider the area around your home as its territory but as what is known as its home range. A cat's home range differs from its territory in that it will share this space with other cats. So if you introduce your cat to another cat on its home range rather than its territory, you will *not* see territorial aggression.

What Should You Expect From An Introduction?

What you should *not* expect to see is the feline equivalents of broad smiles and warm handshakes. Your cat's encounter with other cats will not resemble those between people or between dogs. It might, however, remind you of the final shootout scene from the movie: *The Good, The Bad And The Ugly*, though without the climactic finish. Just because your cat seems standoffish or even hostile when in the presence of other cats, does not mean it isn't still enjoying the encounter.

Cats have unique personalities and there is no way to tell exactly how your cat will react when introduced to another cat, and vice versa. But the odds of a successful interaction are raised if both cats are individually sociable animals. If your cat was not well socialized to other cats as a kitten, it will not be as bold in social encounters as would a well socialized cat. Your cat will be more cautious, need more space, and it will take longer for your cat to feel comfortable around the other animal.

Trying is the only way to find out if your cat will benefit from being introduced to other cats. If your cat seems stressed and irritable after returning from visits, this activity might not be suitable for it.

How Do You Introduce Your Cat To A Friend's Cat?

Before you begin, it is necessary that your cat is familiar with and feels comfortable around your friend, and also that your friend's cat feels comfortable around you. The next step is to take your cat to your friend's yard, but have them keep their cat indoors. Walk your cat in the same places where your friend usually walks his or her cat. You will notice that your cat will be aware of and show a strong interest in the places that your friend's cat has been. The next time your friend takes their cat for a walk, it will readily pick up on the scent marks left by your cat. And there it is! Your cat and your friend's cat are on their way to getting to know each other.

Repeat this process until your cat is comfortable walking in your friend's yard as we described in the section Familiarity earlier in this chapter. It is important to make sure that your cat feels safe *before* it is brought face-to-face with the other animal. Then, it is time for the cats to become a little more acquainted.

Your goal now is to accustom the two cats to each other's presence. Bring both cats out and have them walk in sight of each other. They might growl or hiss softly—or completely ignore each other. When it is clear that they have seen each other, have them sit in each others presence until they begin to relax.

As a general rule, keep the cats about six feet apart unless they are completely comfortable around each other. And if they do approach each other more closely than this, make sure you watch them for aggressive body language (see chapter 8, Learning Catanese). While an attack is unlikely, it could happen. So make sure to keep the cats out of claws' reach.

Over a period of several visits, repeat this process, letting them gradually get closer to each other. It is important to remember that cats need their personal space, and some cats will need more than others. We discuss this process of accustoming cats to each other, and to other things, in more detail in chapter 7. Once the cats are familiar with each other, you and your friend can walk them at the same time in the places you had previously walked them individually.

Walk Your Cat

Leash-Training: Part 1

In this chapter, we will show you how to properly handle your cat as it ventures outdoors. Earlier, we indicated that improper handling of your cat on a walk will create conflict and make walking it impossible. Conflict can also arise if, for whatever reason, your cat refuses to cooperate with you. As you will see, when your cat refuses to do what you want, it will do so in only one of a few ways. So dealing with conflict with your cat is simply a matter of detraining these few common refusal behaviors.

Like many cat owners, you might face resistance from your cat when you try and put a harness on it. If this is the case, eliminating conflict will begin even before you open the door to take your cat out.

> By putting a harness on your cat, you are making it less able to protect itself. This is the reason why cats often react violently to having a harness put on them.

How To Put On Your Cat's Harness (without being scratched or bitten)

To overcome your cat's resistance to wearing a harness, you must teach it to associate having its harness put on with the activity of going outside. You will make your cat understand that the *only* way it can go outdoors is with its harness on. Once your cat understands this, you will find that it will be quite cooperative with you when you put its harness on it.

You can inform your cat that going outdoors is possible by giving it some exposure to the outdoors, as described in chapter 3. After doing this, your cat will begin showing interest in the door when you open it, so be careful not to let it escape. Once your cat shows interest in going outdoors, the next step is to get it harnessed up.

Walk Your Cat

When your cat comes to the door, try to put its harness on it. If it offers significant resistance, give up for the moment, let it calm down and try again later. *The calmer, or even sleepier, your cat is, the easier it will be to put a harness on it.* By backing down temporarily you are avoiding an unnecessary confrontation with your cat. Your cat will come to understand that resisting having its harness put on results in it not going out and that if it allows you to put its harness on, it can go outdoors.

> Food treats are an obvious reward you can use to train your cat. However, when it comes to training your cat to be walked, and in particular to putting its harness on it, you will be hard pressed to find anything your cat desires more than going outside. So, to get it into its harness without a fuss, you will be much better off having your cat directly make the association between wearing its harness and the activity of going outside than rewarding it using treats or other incentives.

As we stressed in Training Tools, it is important to make a clear connection between a behavior you are training and the reward you are using to train that behavior. In this case, you must make the connection between the harness and the outdoors very clear for your cat. Here are some steps you can take to achieve this:

- ☑ *Never take your cat outdoors without its harness on.*

Leash-Training: Part 1

- ☑ *Once you have put your cat's harness on it, don't delay in taking it outdoors.*

- ☑ *Take the harness off immediately after returning indoors.*

- ☑ *Make sure the harness fits comfortably.*

The last item on this list needs some explanation. If the harness is too tight, your cat will understandably resist having it put on. Being uncomfortable distracts your cat from being able to make the desired association between its harness and the pleasant activity of going outdoors. If you find that your cat resists having its harness put on, the first thing to check is whether its harness is too tight. On this point, it is worth mentioning that harnesses can mysteriously shrink over time, so it is a good idea to routinely check the fit of your cat's harness.

To check that the harness fits correctly, make sure you can slip two fingers snugly between the collar and your cat's neck and again between the torso strap and your cat's body. Straps that fit snugly will make it harder for your cat to free itself and are also less likely to snag on an object as your cat walks by it. However, if you have difficulty putting the harness on, consider loosening the straps, which will make it easier to put on.

Once your cat is trained and walks are a routine part of its life, it can be easy to become lax with regards to the four points listed above. Be careful not to let this happen. Your cat wants to be outdoors, but would prefer to do so without its harness and without you leading it around. It wants to have its cake and eat it too. As a result, your cat can become conflicted about wearing its harness, which it doesn't like but which is associated with something it does like—going outdoors. The harness can become a source of anxiety for your cat. If this happens, your cat will come running when you signal it to go out, but then will refuse to come near the door for you to put its harness on. But if you follow the four suggestions above, wearing a harness outdoors will become second nature to your cat.

Where To Stand In Relation To Your Cat

Always stand to the *side and rear* of your cat, as shown in the picture below. This position has several advantages over possible alternatives. First, it ensures that when you or your cat pull on the leash, the pressure exerted is directed more towards your cat's torso than to its neck. Second, your cat will prefer this

arrangement as having you stand behind it allows it a clear view of its surroundings without your blocking its view. Having an unobstructed field of vision is important for your cat who, when outdoors, will always be on the lookout for danger and potential prey. Finally, as you will see in the next chapter, standing to the side and rear of your cat is the best position for directing your cat using the leash.

Handling The Leash

Being able to get along with your cat outdoors is an important factor for success in training it to walk on a leash. Since the leash is the main way you will communicate with your cat when walking it, getting along with it means, first and foremost, handling its leash correctly. Below we provide guidelines that will help ensure that your cat will be happy to walk with you when you take it outdoors.

Be gentle with the leash. The leash is not just a tether to stop your cat from running away. It is also not a tool to force your cat to do what you want it to do. *Dragging your cat or lifting it off the ground using the leash should never be done.* Coercion serves no purpose in leash-training your cat and will only slow or reverse any progress you have made. Remember, force is not a motivator for cats. Only their desire for the outdoors will make them cooperate with you. Furthermore, despite their impressive physical abilities, cats are fragile and can be easily injured by improper handling.

Your handling of the leash should be friendly and encouraging rather than bossy. You can set this tone by handling the leash gently and smoothly. Don't pull hard or jerk on the leash.

Walk Your Cat

Keep your cat on a short taut leash most of the time, as shown in the picture on page 56. Make sure there is no slack on the leash and that you can prevent your cat from walking away from you in any direction. As a general rule, the more control you want to exert over your cat, the closer you will stand to it and the shorter the leash should be.

Along with increasing your control over your cat, maintaining a taut leash also reminds it that your presence is an indispensable part of its walks outdoors. Keeping the leash slack too often will cause your cat to forget this fact and become uncooperative with you when you walk it.

Give your cat some slack. Allowing your cat some freedom, by slackening its leash, is okay whenever your cat is doing one of the natural activities that we described in the last chapter. In particular, when your cat is hunting it will want as much freedom on the leash as you can give it.

But be aware that a longer leash makes it easier for you to lose control of your cat. When your cat is on a long leash, you need to watch it that much more closely for signs it is about to dart off or get into a situation where you cannot quickly regain control.

> Cats have the ability to accelerate rapidly and can easily surprise a distracted owner. A short leash prevents your cat from building up speed, allowing you to keep it safe and under control.

Be predictable. Handling your cat unpredictably will generally be very stressful for your cat and particularly so when you are restraining it on a leash. Handling it in the same way each time you take it out will help your cat know what it can expect from you when it goes out. This will help build trust and habituate your cat to your presence on its walks.

Understand your role. Your role on a walk with your cat is as a guide for your cat and not as its boss. Never try to force your cat to do anything. Instead, use the methods described in chapter 2 to change its behavior.

It can be easy to become overly bossy with your cat, especially if you are in a rush. Therefore, it is a good idea to decide beforehand how much time you will spend outdoors with your cat and plan your walks accordingly, leaving enough time for the return walk home.

Venturing Outdoors

To take your cat outdoors, you will need to first put its harness on. If you have trouble getting your cat's harness on, re-read the section How To Put On Your Cat's Harness (without being scratched or bitten), **earlier in this chapter.** As we discussed there, only when your cat comes to the door should you put its harness on it. Then immediately open the door, and allow it to walk out.

Your cat may not automatically run outside, but instead may loiter near the door. Like dipping one's foot in a swimming pool before jumping in, your cat will want to cautiously feel out the new environment before it goes too far out. This is true when letting your cat outdoors for the first time, and also when taking it somewhere it has not been before.

Once your cat does venture out, it may want to return home quickly. This does not mean it doesn't like going outdoors.

Walk Your Cat

These early trips are important confidence-building experiences for your cat, who will be emboldened by them and become eager for more. You should view any trip outdoors, no matter how short, as a successful trip.

> An added benefit of regularly walking your cat is that it will become familiar with the area around your home. So if it ever manages to get out of your home, it will be less likely to become disoriented and get lost.

Knowing that it has a safe place to run to if it suddenly finds itself in danger will help your cat feel secure on its walks. If possible, leave your door ajar when you step outside, so your cat understands it can go back in whenever it wants. Otherwise, always be prepared to open the door quickly when your cat wants to go back inside. Once your cat does go in, remember to take its harness off immediately to help your cat reinforce the association between wearing a harness and going out.

For the first few trips outdoors, limit your control over your cat as much as possible. Your cat will need time to become accustomed to the outdoors and to walking on a leash with you before you begin training it to respond to your directing it. If at any point your cat decides it wants to sit rather than walk, let it do so. Sitting gives it time to familiarize itself with the area around it. And when it does walk, let it go where it wants to, but use the leash to prevent it from going anywhere you could potentially lose control of it. Don't let it crawl under bushes, through holes in fences or climb into the branches of a tree.

> Try walking your cat along a visibly distinct path, such as a sidewalk or a trail. Cats will naturally follow paths, so it will be easy to have your cat follow one.

You may be tempted to try and haul your cat off to the far reaches of your garden after only a couple of trips out. This is not a good idea and can be stressful for your cat. When your cat is ready to do some exploring and move farther from home, you can be sure it will let you know.

On its own, your cat might avoid certain places solely because it has not been in them before. You can actively encourage your cat to walk in these places by using the reassurance techniques you will learn in chapter 7, The Art Of Reassurance. Once your cat gains experience walking in an area, it will be less resistant to walking there in the future.

Your cat will always be more comfortable and more cooperative with you when you are walking it in familiar places where it feels safe. A good strategy to accommodate your cat's natural sense of caution is first to restrict its walks to the same paths or small area until it feels comfortable there, then you can begin to make small detours. In this way, you can gradually enlarge the area you walk your cat in.

Once your cat is used to being walked and has an established walking area, you can begin to take it off the beaten path. Consider taking it to a new park or for a walk in the woods. But keep in mind the restrictions on locations for walking your cat that we discussed in chapter 4.

Dealing With Conflict

There will be times while walking your cat, when it will refuse to do what you want it to do. As we have said, getting into a test of wills with your cat is counterproductive. A more effective way to get your cat to cooperate is to train it not to refuse in the first place. By doing this, you can avoid conflict and still get your cat to do what you want.

Recognizing Conflict

Because your cat will be more motivated to go outdoors than to return inside, from time to time you are likely to face resistance from your cat when returning indoors after a walk. You will gently pull on the leash but your cat will resist, having decided that it would rather stay out. It strains against the leash and hisses, grumbles, or vocalizes its annoyance to you in its own unique way. It may even try to bat your leg with its paw.

Believe it, or not, none of these behaviors are actually signs that your cat is refusing to cooperate with you. They are just your cat's way of attempting to convince you to let it stay outdoors. If your cat could speak, it would instead say: "You're not the boss of me. I really want to stay out, so back off!" While your cat does have a point, with a little care, you can still get it to back down without the situation escalating into a confrontation.

Your cat will only *truly* refuse to do what you want when it has reached the limits of its patience with you. Some signs

Leash-Training: Part 1   **63**

that your cat is really refusing to cooperate with you are: it tries to back out of its harness; it crouches to the ground and stiffens its body becoming a little furry statue; or it slumps to the ground or lies down, often on its side, so as to be a dead weight and will not get up without being dragged. Additionally, on rare occasions, your cat might become extremely excited or aggressive.

> If your cat finds itself in a situation where it feels threatened, it will want to run away. It will become very aggressive towards you if you try to prevent it from escaping. For this reason, you should be extremely careful when picking your cat up when it is afraid.

How To Train Your Cat Not To Back Out Of Its Harness

Your cat may try to free itself from your control by backing out of its harness. You might think that all you need is a tight harness to stop this behavior. Unfortunately, this is not the case. Having a tight harness may make it somewhat more difficult for your cat to escape but this won't stop it from trying and it can hurt itself if it partially succeeds in getting out of its harness.

A more effective strategy is to train your cat not to even try to back out of its harness. You will convince your cat that attempts to free itself are pointless. This is a safer approach than using a tight harness and also has the advantage of avoiding conflict between you and your cat. How does it work?

Walk Your Cat

As it turns out, without hands or opposable thumbs, your cat's options for freeing itself from its restraint are fairly limited. The only way your cat can succeed is if *you* keep the leash taut while it walks backwards squeezing its head and torso through the straps. The reason your cat walks backwards is that it expects you will pull on the leash in the opposite direction. But if you do not give your cat something to pull against, it will be impossible for it to back out of its harness.

To ensure that your cat feels no resistance, slacken the leash as soon as your cat begins backing up. After repeated attempts your cat will realize that the only thing it is achieving by trying to back out of its harness is to look silly. And it will stop trying.

As we discussed in the section Futility, in chapter 2, you should never give your cat any reason to think that the behavior you are de-training will be rewarded, in this case that backing out of its harness *might* succeed. This is why it is important to slacken the leash the instant your cat puts itself in reverse, and give it nothing to pull against. You will find this easier to do if you are standing to the rear of your cat.

But, you may say: "When my cat walks backwards, isn't it succeeding in walking in the opposite direction that I want it to?" That may be so, but this is not the reason your cat is walking backwards. Usually it will stop after a short distance if it feels no resistance on the leash. However, if it keeps walking backwards, you should pick it up and put it back where it started.

Once your cat learns that backing out of its harness achieves nothing, it will stop doing it and will resort to other methods to try and get its own way.

The Dead-Weight Maneuver

Another way that your cat will refuse to cooperate with you that you are likely to see on its walks is what we like to call the dead-weight maneuver. Your cat will slump to the ground, lying on its side so as to be a dead-weight. In this position, your cat has an effective defense—its well positioned claws and teeth—to stop you from picking it up. So how do you get past its defenses and get it walking again without being scratched or bitten? Once again, you will use futility to de-train this behavior.

Every time your cat lies on the ground and refuses to get up, use the leash to slowly lift up its torso, moving its front legs so that your cat ends up in a sitting position with its front legs over its hind legs as shown in the picture below. Once your cat un-

derstands that this defensive method of refusal will not succeed, it will not resist for long when you lift its torso up, as just described, and it will quickly start walking again. If your cat continues to refuse or gets overly excited, you might have to pick it up and carry it indoors.

Taking your cat indoors prevents further conflict with it; however, it also punishes it by shortening the walk. Since it is always better to avoid punishing your cat, carrying it indoors should only be done as a last resort. If your cat refuses to cooperate or gets overly excited, try petting it and giving it a minute to calm down before trying to get it to walk again. Often these time-outs will do the trick.

How To Get Your Cat To Return Indoors After A Walk

The most persistent source of conflict between you and your cat on its walks will be getting it to return indoors. Your cat is strongly motivated to go outdoors, but returning indoors is another story altogether. Learning to direct your cat as described in the next chapter and following the suggestions below will make your cat cooperative when it comes time to go back inside:

Time your walks. Your cat will become used to the duration of your walks. If you regularly take it for long walks, it will be more likely to resist going in after a short walk.

Create a routine. One way to do this is to create a circuit between places you like to take your cat. You can also have several different circuits to add variety and keep things interesting for your cat. Following a fixed circuit provides a natural end to walks.

Leash-Training: Part 1

Rest with caution. On a warm summer day, your cat will really enjoy a long rest in the shade. But be aware that this activity can have the effect of making it harder to get your cat to return indoors willingly. If your cat refuses to walk after a rest, pick it up and carry it away from its resting spot before you continue to walk it home. Then on future walks, avoid that resting spot for a while.

Create a verbal signal to let your cat know that it is time to return indoors. Once you have decided to return indoors, say "Inside" or "Go home," for example, then immediately start heading home. Verbal signals can work against you if, after you have signalled your cat to go indoors, you allow it to delay so that your cat thinks there is a chance it can remain outdoors. In that case, it will interpret "Go Home" as a cue to start delaying going in. Once you inform your cat that it is time to return indoors, make sure your cat understands that there is no possibility *whatsoever* of staying outdoors.

Let it enjoy the trip home. Allow your cat some freedom to do 'cat stuff' as described in chapter 4, as you head indoors. It is important, however, that you don't let it lead you away from home in the process, or purposely delay going in. A good clue that your cat is simply stalling is if it starts looking around as it searches for something of interest, and resists walking.

Argue with your cat. Forcing your cat to be cooperative by dragging it is not an option, so instead try to convince it to go indoors. You can be sure that it will try its best to convince you to let it stay out. It might plead with you vocally or attempt to intimidate you by hissing, growling or lashing out. For your part, you must let it know that you are not affected by its attempts to manipulate you. Pat or stroke your cat and talk calmly to it. Be a little firmer in your handling of the leash and more insistent in leading it indoors. Your cat will respond to this type of interaction.

Associate something positive with going indoors. Give your cat a food treat as soon as you take its harness off when you return indoors. As you do so, say, "Treat" or whatever word you prefer. Your cat will learn to associate the word "Treat" with the food treat. You can then start using the word "Treat" when you are still outdoors (but not too far from the door) to help lure your cat inside. In the event that you have to pick your cat up and carry it indoors, *don't* give it a treat. The treats are meant as a reward for your cat for being cooperative when returning indoors.

If all else fails, pick your cat up and take it indoors if it refuses to walk in on its own. As we have already stressed, punishing your cat by taking it indoors should generally be avoided, but it is a better option than getting into a confrontation with your cat. The effect of prematurely ending a walk is that the next time your cat goes outdoors, it will be less inclined to resist returning indoors after you signal it to do so. Expect that early on in your cat's training, you will from time to time have to pick it up and carry it indoors.

Leash-Training: Part 2

Imagine the following: It's a warm summer day. Your cat waits patiently at the door while you put its harness on. You head outdoors, and as you walk with your cat, it follows your directions, almost obediently, as you take it to different points of interest. Along the way it pauses to investigate its surroundings, intently sniffing the scent marks left by other animals on grass blades, bushes, fenceposts and other objects. You stop to allow it to chew some tender grass and then head over to its favorite log where it enthusiastically scratches its claws. It suddenly darts off to chase a butterfly, which has landed on a nearby flower. You continue on, and after a while you stop to let it rest in the shade. Your cat is invigorated, enjoying the excitement outdoors, the fresh air and the exercise. But then, alas, it is time to return indoors. Your cat goes in quickly even if grudgingly and you say to it, "What a good cat you are" as you shut the door behind it and give it a treat.

In the course of this walk outdoors, you would want your cat to turn left or right, and to start or stop walking. Sometimes you would want it to turn completely around. In the following sections, we will show you how to use the leash as well as verbal cues to control and direct your cat.

Directing Your Cat

With a bit of practice, all it will take will be a gentle tug on your cat's leash to get it to change direction, or to start or stop walking. This method of directing your cat is called *tuggling*. In this section, we will show you how to train your cat to respond to tuggling. Training is accomplished in a series of steps that begins by simply using the leash to prevent your cat from going where you do not want it to go.

The Path Of Least Resistance

Start by taking your cat outdoors, walking to its side and rear and keeping it on a short, taut leash. As you walk with your cat,

Leash-Training: Part 2

it will, at some point, want to walk in a different direction than you want to. When this happens, don't follow your cat, but stand firm and use the leash to prevent it from going in that direction. Follow your cat only if it walks in the *general* direction you want to go in. For example, if you want your cat to walk to the left, don't try and pull it to the left, instead use the leash to prevent it from walking either to the right or forward. Having no other choice, it will walk to the left.

What this achieves is that you are able to direct your cat, even though not very precisely at the moment, without having to pull your cat in the direction you want. Cats don't like being forced to do things and your cat will interpret your pulling on its leash as an attempt to dominate it. If you pull on the leash, your cat will quickly become grumpy and uncooperative. In contrast, by holding the leash taut and letting *your cat* pull on the leash, it will interpret the resistance it feels on the leash as an "act of nature" rather than attributing it to you.

As you might have guessed already, this technique is an application of the method of futility that you were introduced to in chapter 2. You will teach your cat that it is futile to try to walk in a particular direction if it feels a lot of resistance on the leash. Initially it might struggle against the leash to go where it wants, but, in time it will stop doing so. Once your cat understands that there is no possibility of going elsewhere, it will give up and reconsider walking where you want it to.

> If your cat refuses to cooperate by trying to back out of its harness or by balking at moving, use the methods described in the last chapter to detrain these behaviors.

Walk Your Cat

Training your cat using futility takes time, and you will need to be patient and take in stride any resistance your cat offers. Cats are good problem solvers and can be quite creative in trying to get their own way. Your cat, for example, may start walking in the direction you want it to, then a short while later will suddenly try and turn back.

This behavior, which you are likely to see, is an example of your cat using trial and error learning. In other words, your cat is searching for a way to get what it wants. Your cat may stop, look around, try a different direction, then walk a bit in the direction you want. Then it will stop again, look around … . It may repeat this behavior often.

As a result, the pace of your walks, initially, will be slow and halting. Be patient, and before you know it this behavior will stop. Your cat is more interested in going exploring and will not want to spend all its time resisting you. As long as it feels it has some palatable options, it will accept the limits you impose on it using the leash.

If your cat feels you are being too pushy, it may hiss at you, bat your leg, or simply refuse to move. If this happens, let your cat guide the walk for a bit before reasserting your control. We also suggest that if you get into a confrontation with your cat, talk to it calmly and pet it to apologize for having been rude.

You might think that this course of action rewards aggressive behavior. For cats, this is not the case. Showing affection to your cat diffuses a tense situation and removes the motivation for your cat's aggression.

Leash-Training: Part 2

Using futility to train your cat, you will also be able to direct it from a standstill. If your cat has stopped walking, keep the leash taut except when your cat *looks* in the direction you want it to walk in. When your cat looks in the direction you want it to go, immediately slacken the leash so that your cat feels no resistance in that direction. When it starts walking again, it will walk in that direction. At this point, you may be tempted simply to keep the leash taut and only allow your cat to go *exactly* where you want it to. But micro-managing your cat's movements is not a good idea.

There are several reasons why when walking your cat, and especially early on in its training, that it is better to allow it a lot of leeway in where it walks. The first is that it will prevent you from over-controlling your cat and having it become stressed out by its lack of freedom. The second reason sounds like something you might hear in a Kung-Fu movie: For your cat, the journey is often more important than the destination. Cats want freedom to inspect the things they encounter around them during a walk—things that you may not even be aware of. Often, your cat will be drawn to interesting scents, sounds or movements nearby that are out of range of your senses.

Your cat's personality will also affect its preferences for where it wants to walk. Consider, for example, that some cats don't like walking in long grass and would prefer to take a detour while other cats really enjoy weaving their way through the grass.

Your cat will always be thinking about its safety, which will also affect the route it prefers to take. For instance, your cat might want to walk along a hedge or a fence that provides it some side cover rather than walking out in the open. Some flexibility on your part will allow your cat to be relaxed, feel safe and better enjoy its experience outdoors. And having your cat enjoy its walks is important for keeping it motivated during its training.

Tuggling

As your cat gets used to the idea that it is pointless to struggle against the leash, you will start to notice that it changes direction faster when it feels strong resistance on the leash. For example, to direct your cat to the left, you use the leash to prevent it from walking forward or to the right. Your cat learns to recognize that when it feels this resistance it will not be able to walk anywhere but left and it will do so quickly.

When this happens you will no longer have to offer firm resistance for an extended period to prevent your cat from walking in a particular direction. In fact, the brief resistance your cat feels from a gentle tug on the leash will be all it needs to understand that it should change direction.

By gently tugging on the leash, you will be able to suggest a direction to your cat to walk in. This is what we refer to as tuggling. To put this more precisely: *Tuggling is a brief gentle tug on the leash that causes your cat to change the direction in which it is looking.* Tuggling is the key to directing your cat because cats (unlike humans) will only walk in the direction they are looking.

A gentle tug to the left will cause your cat to look to the left, and a gentle tug to the right will cause it to look to the right. To get your cat to turn a little more to the left or to the right, you will use slightly more force when you tug on the leash. The connection between how you tuggle your cat and where your cat looks is something your cat will learn from experience.

THE TUGGLING CHECKLIST

☑ The first step in training tuggling is to prevent your cat from walking anywhere but in the most general direction you want it to walk in.

☑ Never try to pull your cat in any direction. Tuggling your cat will cause it to change the direction it is looking in. *It will then walk on its own in that direction.*

☑ When you tuggle your cat, the only part of its body that should move is its head.

☑ Tuggling is most often done by gently pulling on the leash sideways or diagonally with respect to your cat's body. This is preferable to pulling your cat backwards or forwards, which cats do not like at all.

☑ Tuggling is easiest to do if you stand to the side and rear of your cat. Depending on where you are standing in relation to your cat, you may first have to reach over your cat's body before tuggling it.

☑ If occasionally your cat doesn't respond when you tuggle it, simply go back to the first step in the process for training tuggling described in the section: The Path Of Least Resistance.

Go

Another application of tuggling is to get your cat to start walking if it has stopped and you are ready to move on. When your cat stops to inspect something during a walk, it might become completely absorbed in whatever has caught its attention. Since the purpose of walking your cat is to let it enjoy such experiences, you should avoid breaking its concentration, but instead wait for it to lose interest before trying to get it to move on.

The telltale sign that its attention has shifted is that it will start looking around. So that is your cue to signal your cat to start walking. To do this, gently pull your cat *sideways* a few inches away from the object that had captured its attention, then tuggle it so that it looks in the direction you want it to walk in. In the same way your cat learned to change directions, it will learn to interpret a gentle sideways tug on the leash when it has stopped as a sign to move on.

Rotate

You can tuggle your cat to get it to change direction or start walking when it has stopped. But tuggling won't do the trick for turning your cat completely around or for making large changes in direction. For these, you will have to rotate your cat. Since the harness is attached to its upper torso near its front legs, pulling on the leash sideways will cause your cat's head and shoulders to rotate about its hind legs. The action is something like opening a door using a string tied to the door knob. When you rotate your cat, you should do it gently and slowly so that your cat won't lose its balance. Watch its hind legs to make sure they are moving in place and that you are not dragging your cat.

Your cat will learn to recognize this turning maneuver and when you begin to rotate your cat, it will complete the turn around on its own. How will your cat react to being rotated? Cats don't like being forced to walk, but your cat will not resist being rotated provided you do it gently.

Wait

For various reasons, you will want your cat to stop and wait for you during a walk. To do this, use the leash to slowly bring your cat to a stop. Once your cat has stopped walking, gently pull back with a little more force on the leash, *then wait* until your cat sits or lies down. The idea here is not to try and pull your cat into a sitting or lying position, but rather to let your cat sit on its own when it feels you pull back on the leash. Consequently you should use very little force when you pull on the leash.

You want to teach your cat the association between sitting or lying down and you pulling gently back on the leash after it has stopped. In this case, you are not using futility, but instead are using a reward to train the association. What is the reward? It is the activity of resting itself! As we mentioned in the chapter Where & When To Walk Your Cat, resting is one of your cat's favorite activities. Because of this you will easily be able to get your cat to sit by signalling it with the leash.

What if your cat doesn't want to sit? Don't try and force it. More often than not your cat *will* want to, and it is at these times it will learn the association between you pulling back on the leash and it sitting or lying down. Once this behavior is learned, your cat will usually sit or lie down when you gently pull back on the leash after you have stopped it.

Controlling Your Cat

Occasionally on a walk, your cat might come across something that interests it, but that you want to keep it away from. Using the leash, you would understandably try to lead your cat away from the object. If your cat is very motivated to reach it, which would be the case if the object it was interested in investigating was a small animal, for example, your cat might struggle fiercely against the leash.

By standing firm and being insistent in not letting your cat get closer to the object you are teaching your cat that it is futile to struggle against the leash. Doing this consistently will train your cat never to struggle against the leash. You want your cat to know that it has no chance whatsoever of overcoming the resistance on the leash. Therefore, once you decide not to let your cat go somewhere, it is important that you stick to your decision.

> The next two sections discuss vocal cues, which depend on you already having trained your cat to respond to the leash signals described in previous sections in this chapter. Therefore, if you want, you can skip ahead to page 84, and return to these sections once your cat is responding well to leash signals.

Vocal Cues

Telling your cat what you want it to do verbally helps clarify your directions for your cat. Occasionally your cat will not understand what exactly you want it do when you signal it using the leash. If you teach it vocal cues, it will listen for them when it is unsure about what you are telling it using the leash. Vocal cues are also an effective tool in their own right that will make your walks more natural and fluid.

> Getting your cat to understand what you want it to do and getting it to do what you want are two important but very different aspects to training cats. In other words, don't assume that the reason your cat isn't doing what you want is because it doesn't understand what you want it to do.
>
> Getting your cat to understand you is an important step. But then you will have to use the training methods, such as futility described in chapter 2, to actually get it to do what you want.

To teach your cat to respond to vocal cues, you will train it to associate some designated word or phrase with a behavior it *already* knows. For instance, your cat already knows that when you put its harness on it will go outside. Now try this: Every time you take out the harness to put on your cat, say "Outside!" It won't take long for your cat to associate this word with the behavior of going outside for a walk. You can then inform your cat verbally of your intentions to take it out. Your cat will react by running to the door so that you can put its harness on.

Vocal cues can be used with any behavior you have taught your cat. We provide several useful examples of using vocal cues in leash-training below, as well as how to train your cat to respond to them.

Will any words suffice as vocal cues? You can use whatever words you want or else, if you wish, simply make up words, or if you are a talented whistler, even whistle. The important thing is that the words, phrases or sounds you choose should be distinct and clearly recognizable to your cat. Additionally, cats respond better to certain sounds over others. In particular, you might want to choose words with 's', 't' and 'ee' sounds in them. Lastly, you know that talking to your cat in a soft, sweet voice evokes a very different response from it than if you shout at it. So when signalling your cat, use a calm, friendly and encouraging tone of voice.

Some Useful Vocal Cues

"Let's Go"

You have learned how to get your cat to start walking again after it has stopped by tuggling it. Using vocal cues, you can do the same thing by simply saying, "Let's go." You can train this vocal cue as follows:

Your cat has stopped to scratch its claws, eat some grass or to smell something along your path. You wait for it to look around, then you say, "Let's go!" Then immediately tuggle your cat to inform it that it is time to move on. If you do this every time you want to move on after a stop, your cat will begin to start walking after you say, "Let's go" without your having to tuggle it.

Maintaining this behavior is easy. Occasionally, you should tuggle your cat *as* you say, "Let's go." This reminds your cat of the connection between the vocal cue and the leash cue. Because this vocal cue depends on being able to tuggle your cat, you will also have to maintain that behavior as we described earlier. We provide more information later in this chapter on how to maintain your cat's training.

"Slow Down"

Your cat's excessive enthusiasm will sometimes cause it to pull hard against the leash, even to the point of choking. You can train your cat not to do this by *purposely* slowing it down whenever it starts to pull hard against the leash. Saying, "Slow down" and then using the leash to slow your cat down will help clarify your intentions to your cat and get it to react faster to the resistance you offer it on the leash.

This vocal cue is particularly useful if you will walk two cats at the same time, where you will want to keep them walking at the same pace. You will, however, need to train each cat to respond to a *different* word as a signal to slow down in order to avoid confusion.

"Stop"

Since you stop your cat in the same way that you get it to slow down, saying, "Stop" to your cat when you want it to stop will help it understand that what you want it do is stop walking altogether rather than just slowing down. To get your cat to stop walking, say, "Stop!" then apply enough resistance on the leash to slowly bring it to a standstill.

Once your cat has learned this cue, it will stop promptly after you give the cue. Because your cat will occasionally not be interested in stopping, you may sometimes still have to use the leash to stop it. As with the cue to slow down, saying, "Stop" allows your cat to avoid choking itself on the leash before it understands what it is you want it to do.

"Wait"

To train this vocal cue, say, "Wait" every time you use the leash to get your cat to sit or lie down, as described earlier in this chapter. It is important that you say, "Wait" just before you signal your cat with the leash. Your cat will learn to associate this cue with it sitting or lying down and will usually do so when you signal it. It will then enjoy resting for a while until you signal it to move on.

"Turn Back"

When your cat walks somewhere, say under a table or bush to inspect something, and you want it to turn back rather than continuing through, you will use the rotation maneuver we discussed earlier. To train your cat to turn around when it hears you say, "Turn back," say it whenever you are about to use the leash to rotate your cat. Once learned, your cat will begin turning around when you say, "Turn back" but before you use the leash to signal it to turn it around.

Leash-Training: Part 2

You can maintain this behavior by occasionally using both the vocal cue and the leash *at the same time* to rotate your cat.

"Inside"

When it is time to return indoors, say, "Inside!" Then immediately head home. As you do so, you should allow your cat to stop and smell plants, eat grass, or scratch its claws, provided it does these on the way to your door. This cue is useful, but can backfire if you allow your cat to lead you way from home after saying it. It will then understand the word "Inside" as a signal to begin resisting going indoors.

"No"

Saying, "No" generally doesn't work with cats. As we mentioned, having your cat understand what you want it to do and having it actually do it are two very different things. To get your cat to respond when you say, "No", you must use futility to teach it *to associate the word 'no' with the resistance it feels on the leash*. Whenever you use the leash to stop your cat from doing something, crawling under a bush, for example, say, "No." Your cat will learn that when it hears the word 'no', it will have no chance of doing what it had wanted to. Note that saying, "No" to your cat when it is not on its leash will detrain this association.

If your cat stops responding to any of the vocal cues described above, the reason is probably that your cat no longer associates the vocal cue with the behavior that it was originally associated with. For instance, if you were to occasionally say, "Outside" to alert your cat that you will take it for a walk, and then not take it out, the word will loose its meaning for your cat. You can retrain the association between the word 'outside' and the activity of going outside by taking it out promptly whenever you say, "Outside."

Sometimes, you can also inadvertently cause your cat to associate a vocal cue with a different behavior. For instance, if you often say, "Outside" then delay taking your cat out, the word 'outside' will come to mean "Not now" for your cat. In this case, it is easier to retrain the correct association using a *new* vocal cue than trying to strengthen the association with the old word. You can begin announcing, "Walk," to your cat, for instance, whenever you take your cat out to have it associate going out with the new word 'walk.'

Teaching your cat to respond to vocal cues builds on behaviors you have already taught it. Because of this, maintaining your cat's response to vocal cues depends on your having maintained the original behaviors on which they are based. The next section summarizes the main issues you need to be aware of for keeping your cat responsive to all of its training.

Maintenance

When your cat is walking well it will be as graceful as cats are known to be. It will be very responsive to your guidance and be very cooperative. At these times, you may be tempted to give your cat a little too much freedom and it can be easy to develop bad habits in handling your cat. You also might begin sending your cat mixed messages when you communicate with it. The result is that your cat will begin to forget its training.

Leash-Training: Part 2

If this happens, you will notice your cat becoming less cooperative and seeming to work against you rather than with you. And if things begin to go really badly, your cat may begin refusing to cooperate with you entirely and will slump to the ground and refuse to move, or try to back out of its harness.

So what should you to do if things go bad? The foundation of your cat's training is teaching it not to refuse to cooperate with you. In chapter 5, Leash-Training: Part 1, we explained how to deal with situations where your cat refuses to cooperate. After that, maintenance involves making sure that you are heeding the lessons of previous chapters. Ask yourself the following questions:

- ☑ Is your cat's motivation high? Are you being careful not to be bossy with your cat? Are you allowing it the opportunity to do the things it enjoys doing outdoors, which we described in chapter 4?

- ☑ Does your cat feel safe on its walks? If not, refer to chapter 7, which explains how to accustom your cat to the places you take it.

- ☑ Are you standing to the side and to the rear of your cat and keeping the leash short and taut *most* of the time?

- ☑ Are you being consistent with the messages you are giving your cat? Or do you occasionally give in to your cat after you have signalled it using the leash, or with a vocal cue, to do something it would rather not do? If you are, this is one reason why your cat is becoming less responsive.

☑ Are the associations between the rewards you give your cat and the behaviors you are training clear for your cat? For instance, does your cat strongly associate its harness with going outside as described in chapter 5?

The last thing to remember about maintaining your cat's training is that training is an ongoing process. For one thing, it is natural for your cat to test you occasionally to see if it can avoid doing what you want it to. Also, if you don't take your cat for walks for an extended period of time, during bad weather for instance, you should expect that you will have to spend some time retraining it when you begin taking it out again. However, retraining the behaviors it forgets will be much easier and faster than when you first taught them.

Walking Two Cats At A Time

You have probably heard the expression: "As difficult as herding cats," which is sometimes used to express the difficulty in coordinating a group of people. But if you have more than one cat and each of them is responding very well to its training, you have the opportunity to show that herding cats—two of them, at least—is actually not that difficult.

Walking two of your cats at a time requires a bit more concentration and effort than walking your cats individually. You will now have to keep a vigilant eye on two cats rather than just on one, and coordinate their movements. Your cats will not help you in this regard, as on walks it will often seem that they are intent on walking in opposite directions. Below are some tips for walking two cats at the same time:

- ☑ Do not try and walk two cats together if they are not each well trained separately. It will be difficult for you to control both of them and the conflict that will result will leave a bad taste in your cats' mouths and yours.

- ☑ It is especially important that both cats are comfortable and familiar with the places you walk them. Walk them along paths and in areas they are individually used to walking in. If either cat is feeling uneasy about its environment, it will be hard to walk them together.

- ☑ Keep them both on a short taut leash but allow enough space between them. Remember, your cats will need some personal space, even though they know each other.

- ☑ To keep them walking at the same pace, you will need to able to slow them down and to bring them to a stop. If one of your cats is inspecting a plant or scratching its claws, you will need to make the other cat wait. To do this, you should teach them vocal cues for slowing down, stopping, and waiting or resting, as described earlier in the chapter. However, you will need to teach each cat a different word for these commands to avoid confusion.

Walk Your Cat

- ☑ When first taking them out together, allow one cat to walk where it wants to for a short while, and have your other cat follow it. Then switch roles and have the first cat follow the other one.

- ☑ When directing your cats, it is a good strategy not to try and direct both cats simultaneously. Deal with one cat at a time. Tuggle one first to change direction, then the other.

- ☑ Safety is a particular concern when walking two cats. If an approaching dog (or a friend of yours) startles both cats, what will you do? They might try and flee in opposite directions. It is important to plan in advance how you will handle such situations. For instance, you might want to pick one cat up and hurriedly direct the other to safety.

Walking two cats can be challenging, especially if your cats individually are not responding well to their training. But if you follow the methods described in this book, and are disciplined and patient, walking two of your cats at the same time can be almost as easy as walking them individually. Furthermore, being able to walk two of your cats together at the same time is a good goal to set when training your cats. If you are able to walk two of your cats together at a time, it is a clear sign that you have succeeded in all the aspects of training cats to walk on a leash that we have laid out in this book.

CHAPTER 7

The Art Of Reassurance

Cats are naturally cautious animals. Their cautiousness is a valuable asset that helps protect them, but at times on walks, it can slow you down to a snail's pace. You will notice this when you first begin walking your cat, since you will be taking it to unfamiliar places where it has not yet learned to feel safe. In this chapter, you will learn how to help your cat become comfortable outdoors more quickly. You do this using simple techniques that are based on the ways that cats normally learn to feel safe. They do so by the processes of *habituation* and *desensitization*.

Your ability to help your cat become accustomed to the outdoors depends on your having a strong bond with it and your ability to reassure it when it is nervous or uncertain. How much reassurance your cat will need on its walks will depend on its personality. Your cat's personal history—its experiences over the course of its life—and to a lesser extent its genes, determine how confident or timid an animal it is. If your cat is a bold adventurer who perhaps has spent considerable time outdoors, it will be more confident and will need less reassurance than if it is a timid or shy cat that has never been outside.

Over time, as your cat becomes an old pro at being walked, it will become comfortable outdoors and need little reassurance. But even then, there will inevitably be times when its cautiousness will disrupt its walks as any environmental change to the places you take it—caused perhaps by rain or snow or new construction—will be disconcerting to it.

Looking For Signs Of Trouble

You probably know your cat well enough to recognize when something has frightened it. But often on walks you will want to know when your cat is simply nervous or unsure of its surroundings. Consider a typical example.

While on a walk outdoors, your cat's behavior suddenly changes. It resists walking in the direction you want it to go. It either stops walking altogether and balks at attempts to get it to move, or it tries to walk off in a different direction. This behavior may be the result of something your cat has sensed in the direction it was being taken that has made it nervous. But it could also be the case that your cat simply doesn't like where it is being taken, or would prefer to go somewhere else. It may have seen, heard or smelled something nearby that it finds more interesting and wants to go and inspect. How can you tell which of these is the case?

The answer is that you must use your cat's body language to let you know what it is feeling. In chapter 8: Learning Catanese, we explain how to do this. If your cat's body language does, in fact, tell you that it is nervous or afraid, you will need to reassure it using the techniques described in the next section.

Reassurance Techniques

How do you reassure your cat that it is safe? To begin with, your very presence is a source of reassurance for it. It will look to you and take your calmness into account in judging if a particular situation is safe. So if anything unexpected happens on your walks—your cat gets stuck under a bush, for example—try to remain calm. If you become agitated or alarmed, you will make your cat uneasy and more difficult to handle.

You can also actively let your cat know that you think there is no danger nearby by talking to it in a friendly tone. Letting your cat hear your voice is an effective way to reassure it in any situation, whether it has been startled by a sudden noise nearby or by the sight of a stranger approaching.

The reason that talking to your cat is so effective, especially when it has been startled, is that cats do not have good vision for detail and will more likely identify you through the sound of your voice than through visual recognition.

For the same reason, it is also a good idea when you or someone else approaches your cat from a distance to always talk to it. Likewise, if your cat appears hesitant to walk towards someone it knows, have them call out to your cat using its name.

> If you feel you need to urgently take your cat back indoors, it is important that you continue talking to it in a calm tone of voice while you insistently lead it inside. Raising your voice and pulling on the leash can cause your cat to panic!

Vocal communication works very well for reassuring your cat, but sometimes a more hands-on approach is needed. Stroking your cat does more than simply show it your affection. For your cat, being stroked has the same comforting and pleasant sensation that kittens experience when being licked by their mothers.

When your cat appears nervous or hesitant and vocal reassurance doesn't seem to be doing the trick, bend down and rest your hand on its lower back just above the tail, as shown in the picture on the next page. You can also gently stroke its lower back. You will be amazed at how effective this is in reassuring your cat and getting it moving again.

It is important to note that reassurance is useful when your cat is unsure, and not when it is afraid. You will see that the techniques described above work well most of the time, but

The Art Of Reassurance

when they don't, there is a very good reason. If your cat does not respond to your reassurance as you expect it to, it could be because it has become aware of something nearby that it considers threatening and is afraid of. If it hears a large animal rustling in the bushes ahead of you, for example, no amount of petting or sweet talking will get it to walk there.

> It is possible to use vocal cues with the reassurance technique described above. Say, "It's okay" just before you pat your cat on its lower back. Doing this every time will teach your cat the association between the gesture and the vocal cue. This association is maintained in the same way as other vocal cues by occasionally using the vocal cue while reassuring your cat by stroking or patting it.

Habituation

When you first take your cat out, it may be very wary of your parked lawn mower, of a dog barking loudly in a neighbor's yard, or of a jogger running towards you. Even an apple falling off a tree could make it stop dead in its tracks. None of these things pose any real threat to your cat and you will want to train it not to react badly when it encounters them.

Cats learn to feel safe around unfamiliar animals and objects by being repeatedly exposed to them without feeling threatened. This is how they learn that most things they encounter in their daily lives are not a threat to them. This process of learning to feel safe is called *habituation*. By being able to ignore harmless objects, cats no longer have to spend their time and energy worrying about them. This frees their minds to focus on more important and interesting things.

You have almost certainly seen your cat learning by the process of habituation. Perhaps your cat has been very cautious around a new object you have brought into your home. It keeps its distance at first and is very suspicious of the object, taking large detours around it when it passes by it. After several passes, your cat becomes more comfortable around the thing and walks progressively closer to it. Eventually your cat becomes habituated to the object and walks right by it without giving it a second thought.

Habituating your cat to the outdoors involves helping it get the needed exposure to new things it will encounter so that it can learn to feel safe around them. Without having had previous experience with your neighborhood jogger, for instance, your cat has no way of knowing if she is a threat or not. This uncertainty will always be a good enough reason for it to run away. So your job in helping your cat get used to her will be to prevent it from running away whenever she jogs by.

> Cats, on their own, get exposure to new things by first observing them at a safe distance, through accidental encounters, or (for kittens) through guidance from their mothers. A mother cat helps expose her kittens to people and animals. A kitten observes its mother's behavior around different animals allowing it to learn if these species should or should not be avoided. Early habituation to new creatures will make a kitten more comfortable with them for the rest of its life.
>
> Habituation is what makes your cat a calm, confident and sociable creature. But confined indoors, your cat can lose its ability to judge whether the things it sees and hears outdoors, such as passing cars or people, are a threat to it or not. As a result, over time it can become shy, more nervous, and less confident overall. Exposure to the outdoors during walks will help your cat develop a general sense of security. This in turn will improve your walks as you will have to spend less time reassuring it.

Whenever your cat comes across something that makes it nervous during a walk but which you think is harmless, you should use the leash to hold your cat still, reassuring it, as described earlier, until whatever worried your cat has passed or until your cat appears to relax.

The key to habituation is to expose your cat to things that make it nervous *at a distance it is comfortable with*. If you were to try and force your cat to get too close to something that it doesn't trust is safe, it would resist fiercely and the experience would only increase its fear of the object.

Desensitization

Cats quickly learn to avoid anything they have had a bad experience with, or have been frightened by, in the past. They quickly become *sensitized* to these things. Encountering something on a walk that your cat is afraid of could be a show-stopper, with your cat immediately turning on its heels (or the feline equivalent) and fleeing back indoors. This is a good reaction if you encounter something that really is a threat to your cat's safety, but unfortunately, accidental events can cause your cat to become fearful of things that are not really a threat to it. It is these things that you will want to desensitize your cat to.

Desensitizing your cat to something that frightens it works in a similar way to how you would help it become accustomed to new things it encounters on its walks, as we described in the last section. The difference, in this case, is that you will need to take into account that your cat will be truly afraid.

When your cat tries to run away from something that you want to desensitize it to, it is important that you don't allow it to run too far. The only way your cat will be able to get over its fear is by being exposed to whatever frightened it. But this should be done with great care.

The Art Of Reassurance

If you were to try to bring your cat to a sudden and complete stop when your cat is afraid and intent on getting away from whatever frightened it, it will try (and probably succeed) in freeing itself from its harness. So, when your cat wants to run away from something, it is important to gauge how afraid your cat really is before you try and stop it.

To do this, try slowing it down with the leash and see how it reacts. If your cat reacts calmly, then keep slowing it down until you bring it to a stop. But if slowing your cat down appears to excite it, you should allow it to continue to move further away before trying to slow it down again. As you slow it down, try reassuring your cat by talking to it and then stroking it. Also, be sure to keep a good grip on the leash. When cats are afraid, they can pull with surprising strength against the leash.

> If you accidently drop the leash and your cat gets away from you, walk calmly towards it, talking to it so it recognizes you. Don't chase after it. If you were to do this, the noise you would make would scare it and it would continue to run away from you. Besides, cats can run much faster than humans and you would not be able to catch it anyway.

Let's illustrate desensitization with a common example. Say your cat, being frightened by the noise, is afraid of cars passing on a nearby street. Every time a car approaches, your cat attempts to run away. To desensitize your cat to this neighborhood traffic, use the method described in the previous paragraphs to stop your cat from running whenever a car approaches. Once you have stopped your cat, continue reassuring it by patting it, and talking to it. Hold your cat still until the car has passed. Then let it go. At this point, you have successfully exposed your cat to a passing car and your cat is on its way to losing its fear of cars. But don't expect instant results.

You will have to repeat the above process many times before your cat is fully habituated to passing cars. The same will be true with anything you are desensitizing your cat to. Being impatient and trying to rush your cat, by trying to prematurely make it walk too near to something it is afraid of, will only increase its fear and set back any progress you have made. Don't set a time limit for desensitizing your cat. Instead make the process of desensitization a part of the routine of your walks and let your cat learn to feel safe outdoors in its own time.

Loss Of Control

Along with desensitizing your cat to things it is afraid of, you will want to prevent your cat from developing any new fears while it is out on a walk. Traumatic incidents—accidents or encounters with unfriendly animals, for instance—will create lasting fears in your cat. Cats have excellent memories and your cat *will* remember these incidents the next time you take it out.

Events that sensitize your cat are most likely to occur when you lose control of it. For example, if your cat manages to crawl under a bush, getting it out can be very stressful for your cat. You can easily prevent this from happening by *never* allowing your cat to climb under bushes or lawn furniture or under anything else that it might get stuck under, or tangled in, while on

The Art Of Reassurance

a leash. The same applies for allowing it to climb into the branches of a tree.

Being strict with your cat about where it can and cannot go is especially prudent when you and your cat are new at going for walks and before your cat is fully responsive to its training.

Strictly prohibiting your cat from getting into situations where there is any chance of you losing control of it will also help you keep it safe while outdoors. The outdoors is a wondrous and exciting place for your cat, but it is also unpredictable and less safe than indoors

Learning Catanese

Cats communicate vocally with their human companions using a variety of different sounds. But most of what cats communicate to us is silent. Cats use body language and facial expressions, as well as gestures, such as rubbing their bodies against us, to let us know what they are feeling and what they want.

Facial expressions and body language provide a lot of information about what a cat is feeling, but owners often avoid relying on these because they do not understand them very well. However, on walks you will have little choice but to rely on your cat's body language. The reason is that what your cat sees, hears and smells on its walks is very different from what you will see, hear and smell. If you spot a big dog ahead of you, you would be quite right to interpret your cat's sudden desire to head in the opposite direction as fear. But more often than not, the things that scare, anger or attract your cat will be out of range of your senses, and you will not be able to predict its behavior by simply keeping an eye on the surrounding environment. You will need to look to your cat's body language to understand its behavior and anticipate what it is about to do.

Another reason you will find it helpful to understand your cat's body language while on a walk is that cats often react to the things they see around them in ways that we find surprising. This happens because cats interpret the world around them in a way that is often alien to humans; therefore, it would be hard to understand and predict their behavior even if you could see, or rather sense, the same things they do.

Your cat may be attracted to things you find disgusting and be terrified by other things that would never even occur to you as being scary. A stationary lawnmower, for instance, might spook your cat, and if you were not keeping an eye on its body language, you could be surprised by your cat's reaction or mishandle it because you failed to realize that it was afraid.

Why can we communicate with our cats? Despite the difficulties people sometimes have in communicating with their cats, the overall extent to which we can communicate with them is actually quite amazing. The fact that we can is not a coincidence.

Over the millenia, cats have learned that there are benefits to being around, and communicating with humans. Humans, in turn, have equally benefitted from having cats around, most notably, for the control of rodents.

Cats, as a species, have adapted to life with us and have become more sociable and less aggressive creatures. They also display communicative behaviors not seen in wild cats. Your cat's "meow," for instance, will almost always be used only to communicate with you and other people. Cats, in general, do not meow at each other. It is an example of a primarily cat-human communication.

Your Cat's Body Language

Below is a very abridged English-Catanese dictionary for interpreting cat body language, which you can expect to see in your cat when you take it outdoors. When translating your cat's body language, remember the following general guidelines:

Learning Catanese

- ☑ Your cat can display multiple emotions simultaneously.

- ☑ Look at its entire body—head to tail—because individual features on their own may mislead you as to what your cat is really feeling.

- ☑ Watch your cat to see how it reacts to different situations, then look for these reactions to predict its behavior.

"I'm Feelin' Good"

Your cat is calm, relaxed and content if its ears are erect and forward, its whiskers lie sideways and are not bunched together. Its body posture will be square in appearance, with shoulders roughly at the same height as its rear end. Its tail may be down, and relaxed, held slightly above the ground, with the fur on the tail being smooth. Its tail could also be standing up, which is how cats signal to other animals and humans that they are in a friendly mood and are approachable.

Your cat's head is stretched forward, body extended, its front legs are drawn back beneath its shoulders. Its whiskers are pointed forward and fanned out. Its ear muscles are flexed, with its ears erect and directed towards a nearby location where it has heard a noise made by potential prey. Its tail starts to twitch. It lowers its body to the ground, and then edges towards the location almost in slow motion. When in range of its prey, your cat will remain frozen, muscles twitching. Then its tail starts to swish back and forth excitedly, it wiggles its rear end as it digs its back feet into the ground…then it pounces.

Learning Catanese   **105**

Your cat can display a continuous spectrum of body language indicating levels of fear from mild nervousness to terror.

When your cat is uncertain of its environment, though not necessarily afraid, all you may see is your cat becoming a bit tense, moving slowly with only a slight lowering of its body profile. Pay attention to your cat's back legs to see if they are slightly bent, lowering your cats rear end.

When your cat is afraid it stands very still, becomes very tense and alert and it crouches—lowering its body to the ground. Cats, when afraid, will try and make themselves small to try to hide from a perceived threat. Its tail will also be tucked in against its body.

But in some situations, your cat may also raise its head up like a periscope to try and get a better look at whatever alarmed it, while trying to keep the rest of its body close to the ground. Then, depending on what it senses and how close the potential threat is, your cat may either quickly lose interest or else lower its head and stealthily but quickly flee.

There are other circumstances where your cat might adopt this body posture, so pay attention to its facial expressions, which can help you see if your cat is worried about something or not.

When your cat is worried or afraid, its pupils will enlarge. Its ears will be drawn back and flattened against its head and its whiskers will be bunched together against the sides of the face.

> Note that your cat isn't always afraid when its ears are drawn back. It could also be listening to something to its side or behind it. In particular, your cat will often keep its ears turned back towards you when you walk it. Likewise, it might still be afraid even though its ears are not drawn back. Its ears could be forward as it listens for a potential threat.

If your cat has been startled or feels threatened, then along with the body language described above, it will also pull its head and shoulders away from the thing that frightened it in order to protect its head.

Contrary to the general rule that cats make themselves small when afraid, there are times when, even though your cat is afraid, it will try and make itself bigger rather than smaller. If confronted by another animal, your cat may arch its back to make itself look big to try and scare off the animal. But its facial expressions will still reveal that it is afraid.

Your cat can show both fear and aggression at the same time. If it feels it is in imminent danger, you will see your cat display defensive-aggressive body language.

'I'm Getting Angry! Really, Really Angry!'

Your cat is displaying aggression towards another animal if it tries to make itself appear big as it attempts to frighten its foe. It will do this by straightening its legs and lifting its rear in the air so that its back is raised above its head level. It will also arch its back to further exaggerate its size. Your cat also expresses anger with its tail, which will have a distinctive arch at the base. The tail will also lash slowly from side to side.

Your cat's pupils will constrict and it will stare intently at its target. Your cat's ears will lie flat against its head, though they will not be drawn back as is the case when it is afraid. Cats lay their ears flat against their head to protect them in anticipation of a fight in which they risk being injured.

> Why does your cat become aggressive? Cats would rather run from a confrontation than risk a potentially dangerous fight. But in the event that something your cat is afraid of manages to get too close for comfort, your cat will become aggressive in order to protect itself.
>
> Cats also display aggression for a variety of other reasons. For instance, if your cat's personal space is invaded by another cat, it may lash out at the intruder even though it does not feel threatened. Your cat may also become aggressive if it is irritated or as an emotional outlet that results from it being stressed.
>
> At times on a walk, your cat may feel you are being too bossy and it may express its annoyance by hissing or growling or lashing out at you. These displays are normal cat behavior and merely its way of telling you to back off. Don't interpret them as bad behavior on your cat's behalf. The best way to respond to displays of aggression from your cat is to take a time-out from whatever you were doing with it. Give it affection, some freedom and time to calm down.

Health & Safety **109**

CHAPTER 9

Health & Safety

When walking your cat outdoors, you could be exposing it to many of the dangers that helped you decide to keep it indoors in the first place. There are also new dangers that your cat faces because it is restrained on a leash. Being aware of these dangers will help you to protect your cat. The information in this chapter will help you to do this. Since we cannot hope to discuss every possible danger your cat could face while on a walk, this chapter, instead, will alert you to some of the major issues that affect your cat's safety while outdoors. The actual risks to your cat and the measures you can take to protect it will depend on where you walk your cat and the particular circumstances in your area, including local disease and insect risks. Therefore, it is a good idea to talk to your vet about possible risks and preventative measures you can take before taking your cat outdoors.

Heatstroke

Cats can sit for long periods of time on what we humans would consider an uncomfortably hot surface. They can do this because they can tolerate a much greater range of temperatures than we can. This, however, does not mean that your cat can spend a lot of time running around in the sun.

While outdoors your cat is susceptible to heatstroke. Unlike humans, cats do not have sweat glands in their skin. As a result, their bodies do not regulate temperature very well, so the temperature of the environment they are in is important. When they need to cool down or warm up, cats will move to a cooler or warmer place. Since you will be controlling your cat's movements, it is important that on hot days you pay close attention to it for signs of heatstroke.

Your cat's mood can help you recognize when it is becoming uncomfortable outdoors. If your cat starts to feel hot, it will likely become irritable. So if you are walking outdoors on a hot day and your cat becomes irritable for no apparent reason, it might be because it is getting too hot and would like to move into the shade.

When your cat experiences extreme discomfort, and in particular when it is overheated, it will pant. If your cat starts panting, you should take immediate action. To help it cool down, move it into the shade where the temperature will be cooler. Rubbing cool water into the fur on its head and back will help cool it down. In extreme cases of heatstroke, you can dip your cat's entire body in cool (not ice-cold) water. You should also immediately take your cat to the vet. Prevention, of course, is better than cure. The best way to keep your cat from becoming overheated is not to take it out in very hot weather.

Sunburn

Cats can get sunburned. This is especially true for light-colored cats and those with thin coats. It may be a good idea to talk to your vet about sunburn risks for your cat before taking it out. Frequent sunburns can lead to skin cancer.

The first sign of skin cancer is a sore on your cat's skin. If your cat has a sore that remains for over a week, particularly on its ears or nose, take it to a vet. It is possible to purchase sunscreen especially made for cats. You should never use sunscreens (or other products) intended for humans, or other animals, on your cat as they can be dangerous for it. This is because a cat's physiology is very different from ours (and because cat's tend to lick themselves).

To reduce your cat's risk of sunburn, you will want to walk it at times when the sun is less intense. In particular, avoid walking it at mid-day during summer months.

Poisons

Cats can absorb poisons through their paws from the surfaces they walk on and also by ingestion while grooming. Therefore, you should always be aware of what your cat is walking on. If you walk your cat on your lawn, check the safety instructions on any chemicals you have applied to it.

Additionally, you should prevent your cat from eating grass and plants that have been treated with pesticide or fertilizer. While cats will usually avoid eating naturally poisonous things, man-made substances, that contain pesticides and other poisons, can thwart their generally good instincts for avoiding things that are harmful to them.

Man-made items that could poison your cat are thawing salts, antifreeze/automobile coolant, rat poison, slug bait, mothball fumes, and many household cleaning products, to name but a few. Rather than trying to remember all the products that are dangerous to your cat, simply keep your cat away from anything that you don't know for sure is safe for it. Keep in mind that not all things that are safe for humans are safe for cats. Chocolate is a good example of this.

Many house and garden plants are poisonous to cats. Azaleas, bluebells, clematis, daffodils, delphinium, lilies, lupine, and poinsettia are some of the plants that are poisonous to your cat. Before allowing your cat to chew on any plant, first find out whether it is poisonous or not. You can do this by looking for pictures of common plants in your area on the internet, or by taking a large enough sample of the plant to a local nursery, home and garden center, or local cooperative extension office and asking them to identify it.

Health & Safety

How can you tell if your cat has been poisoned? Some signs of poisoning are drooling, fast breathing (cats breathe normally at about twice the rate of humans), severe nausea, abdominal pain, diarrhea, rapid or irregular heart beat (a cat's normal heart rate is roughly twice that of humans), muscle tremors, staggering, seizure, and coma.

If you suspect your cat has been poisoned, immediately call your vet or the fee based ASPCA National Animal Poison Control Center Hotline (1-888-426-4435).

> It is a good idea to post the number above, as well as your vets number, in an easy to find location because minutes are important in cases of poisoning.

Insects

Going outdoors increases your cat's exposure to fleas, ticks, mosquitoes and stinging insects. Stings can be serious for some cats who might have an allergic reaction. A sting on the mouth can be especially problematic, as it can result in obstruction of your cat's breathing.

Fleas pose a less urgent problem, but one that you don't want to ignore. If you notice any fleas, we recommend that you deal with this problem promptly, or it could quickly grow to make your cat's life and your's miserable. Getting rid of a few fleas is a lot easier than the large population that will result if the problem is left untreated. Your cat can also get tapeworms from eating fleas. Brushing your cat after walks will help control fleas (and ticks). There are also a large number of products on the market for killing fleas.

In North America, mosquitoes do not pose the health risk to humans that they do in many other parts of the world. But they can be deadly for your cat. They can transmit heartworm larvae to it, which can lead to a fatal heartworm infection. While indoor cats are also known to contract heartworms, the risk of your cat getting heartworms increases when you take it outdoors. Heartworms are difficult and expensive to treat, so prevention is important. Infection can be prevented with heartworm disease preventive products that are available for cats. The risk of heartworms is higher in some parts of the country than others, so you will need to check online or ask your vet to see if you live in a high risk area.

You can also help protect your cat by adjusting the times and locations of your walks. Mosquitoes, which can be present at all times of the day, are more prevalent at dawn and dusk and around standing water (shallow puddles and water-filled containers, for example).

Diseases & Parasites

The risks from diseases, like the risks from insects, vary depending on where you live. Ask your vet about vaccinations and other preventive measures you can take before you take your cat outside.

The main concerns are infectious diseases that your cat can contract when it comes into direct or indirect contact with other animals or prey. Rabies, feline panleukemia, feline infectious

Health & Safety **115**

peritonitis, feline leukemia, and feline immunodeficiency virus are examples of common transmittable feline diseases. Cats can be vaccinated against rabies, feline panleukemia, and feline leukemia. There is no vaccine for the feline immunodeficiency virus.

Your cat can contract a disease if it comes into close contact with another animal, shares the same water source, or is scratched or bitten. As stimulating as it may be for your cat, it is also best not to let it nose about in the fecal matter of other animals. Though this is one form of social communication for cats, fecal matter can contain and transmit various diseases, including feline leukemia.

Your cat can get various parasites and worms from eating many of the animals you might encounter on a walk outdoors, including mice, shrews, birds, lizards, toads, geckos and earthworms. If your cat catches a mouse or other animal, it is best to take its prize away.

General Safety Issues

Restraining your cat on a leash allows you to keep it out of trouble. However, the leash prevents your cat from relying on its lightening fast reactions to get out of the way of danger and therefore limits its ability to protect itself. At the first sign of an approaching dog, your cat would head for the nearest tree. Its leash prevents this, so now it is up to you to take action. Keeping a vigilant eye on the surrounding environment will alert you to potential dangers. But, as we mentioned earlier, you will also have to watch your cat's body language as its keen senses will probably detect any danger before you do.

Walk Your Cat

In reality, your cat should be more concerned about you than any other threat since you will be closest to it on walks. If you (or anyone else) trips over your cat or its leash, it can be seriously injured. As we suggested in chapter 1, a brightly colored or, even better, a fluorescent leash will help reduce the risk of anyone tripping over it.

You also need to take care that your cat doesn't manage to get its leash tangled on something. Your cat will not realize the limitations of being on a leash and harness. When it climbs under a bush, it will not realize that it can become entangled by its leash and harness. A more serious risk is being dangled, or hanged, on its leash. This can happen if, for example, your cat jumps over a high fence while you are holding its leash. So what should you do if this happens? Usually, it is better to let the leash go rather than risk having your cat hanged by it. Of course, it is better not to get into this situation in the first place by never letting your cat surprise you by jumping over fences, or by climbing onto high ledges, or into the branches of a tree.

Below is a summary of things you can do to protect your cat's safety when you take it out on a leash.

- ☑ Always have complete control of your cat.

- ☑ Always keep an eye on what your cat is doing.

- ☑ Pay attention to the environment in which you are walking and to your cat's body language.

- ☑ Have a plan of what to do if things go wrong. If a big dog approaches, or if your cat panics for any reason and wants to run, you should know what you will do in advance.

Health & Safety

☑ Always remember that your cat's safety while on a walk is entirely in your hands and that being on a leash makes your cat less able to protect itself.

CHAPTER 10

Your Cat At A Glance

This chapter will give you a better understanding of your cat, how it sees the world, and its natural behavior. Understanding your cat will help you to avoid misinterpreting its behavior when walking it, and improve your ability to communicate with it. It will also give you better insight into why access to the outdoors is so important to your cat.

Cat Physiology

Body Structure & Mobility

As is the case with most aspects of the domestic cat's physiology, the feline musculoskeletal system evolved for efficient hunting. It gives cats amazing flexibility and mobility. A mature cat can sprint roughly twice as fast as the average human and can jump five times its own body length. Interestingly though, cats have poor endurance, and are not designed for marathon running. A relaxed walk is the most economical way for them to get around. Cats will speed up to a trot when moving long distances, or to a gallop for purposes of hunting and getting away from a perceived danger. Rather than engaging in long chases, cats prefer to sneak towards unsuspecting prey, then use their specially adapted hind legs to pounce on them.

Likewise, to escape a dog that is chasing it, a cat will head for the nearest tree rather than risk being caught up in a long chase. With contortionist flexibility, powerful muscles, excellent balance and sharp, curved claws, cats are excellent climbers. To climb a tree, a cat will leap—a running leap if possible, for the first length—then use its curved needle-like claws to walk up the tree. Cats cannot turn around and walk down a tree, but must back down, jump or be helped down.

The Senses

Cats rely heavily on more of their senses than humans do to make their way around. They use their whiskers, noses, ears, and eyes to paint a mental picture of their environment. All of their senses are, in certain ways, significantly heightened compared to human senses. This helps cats not only in finding and catching prey but also in sensing dangers when they are still far off, allowing cats plenty of time to run to safety.

Vision

Cats have excellent vision though, notably, they cannot see well at very close range. To be able to detect dangers and prey, cats have a very large field of vision. Part of this is peripheral vision—what they see "out of the corner of their eye." If we had comparable vision, we would be able to see backwards over our shoulders.

While outdoors on a walk, what your cat will be paying attention to is not the details of what it sees around it—but movement. Cats, in fact, do not see detail very well but are able to detect even the slightest motion.

The adaptation of your cat's eyes to hunting is seen in that it focuses most sharply on objects that are 7-20 feet away. This is where it has a good chance of catching its prey. Furthermore, cats' eyes function extremely well in low-light conditions in which they prefer to hunt. They need only a small fraction of the amount of light that humans need in order to see. In low-light conditions, your cat will be much better at detecting changes in brightness than in distinguishing colors. Color is less important for cats than it is for humans. When cats look around, the world appears to them as mainly green and blue.

A final adaptation of cats' eyes to hunting is their excellent depth perception, which allows them to accurately gauge their distance from prey that they are chasing. It is also how cats are able to jump long distances and land on very narrow objects without missing.

Hearing

Your cat has a large number of muscles in its ears, which allows it to turn them completely around. And it can do so much faster than any dog can turn its ears. Your cat will more likely identify potential prey, or a potential threat, by hearing it than by seeing it. Because of this, you are better off watching your cat's ears rather than its eyes to know what has caught its attention outdoors.

The structure of your cat's ears allows it to locate prey quickly and accurately by being able to distinguish between sounds that are only inches apart. While hunting, your cat will, with good odds of success, catch prey that is hidden in the grass, which it has accurately located by sound alone.

You will not be able to hear much of what your cat hears. Its hearing is far more sensitive than yours, and it can hear things that are well outside your range of hearing. Your cat will be highly receptive to the high pitched squeak of a mouse and the rustle of an insect in the grass, sounds which you would be oblivious to.

Smell

A cat's sense of smell is many times better than humans and only slightly less sensitive than that of dogs. A cat smells with its nose and with an organ called the vomeronasal organ, located on the roof of its mouth. Your cat will often stop and pause near an object. It will open its mouth slightly and appear to focus intensely. With the help of its vomeronasal organ, your cat paints a smell picture by detecting chemical scents—left, perhaps, by another animal that has recently passed by.

The sense of smell is very important to your cat for socializing with other cats. Cats use scent as a means to communicate. By smelling the scent marks left by other cats, your cat can learn a tremendous amount about them—including information about their diet, health, and sex. Through smell your cat learns the recent history of an area it is in. It can discover whether other animals—possibly friend or foe or food—are or have recently been nearby.

Touch

Like humans, your cat can feel when something is pressing against its body. Its paws are especially sensitive to touch. Your cat can also feel temperature. It knows whether its food is hot or cold, and when it sits by the window, it can feel the warmth of the sunlight shining on it. Cats, however, are much less sensitive to temperature differences than humans are. The exception is your cat's nose, which can detect very small changes in temperature.

Cats also feel with the hair on their bodies. They have special hairs, which stand slightly above the rest of their coat, which are particularly sensitive. With these your cat can feel the wind, or a gentle breeze, and know when some object is brushing against it. Cats feel with their whiskers too, which are found on their cheeks, chin, eyebrows, and on the back of their front legs. Whiskers help orient your cat, allow it to navigate in the dark, gauge the size of small openings, locate objects and protect its body.

Taste

Cats, like humans, can distinguish between acidic, bitter, and salty tastes. But they have a very limited sense of sweet, which is understandable in light of their carnivorous diet.

The Natural Life Of The Modern Domestic Cat

Cats have a long history of living with and around humans. This relationship has helped to make your cat the creature that it is. Still, your cat is much more similar to wild cats than it is different from them. And if you really want to know what makes your cat tick, you must imagine what its life would be like if it lived apart from humans. That is, you must imagine what your cat's life would be like if it left the creature comforts of its indoor life behind and struck out on its own into the great outdoors. Where would it live and spend its time? What would it eat? Would it live alone or in a group? Would it still be the same affectionate, playful creature you know and love? The answers to these questions provide insight into how your cat perceives the world around it.

In its new life outdoors, your cat would want to find a place to live that could support it with a reliable source of food, shelter, security, and social interaction with other cats. Finding a suitable place to live will not be hard for your cat. Cats are very adaptable. They live in environments ranging from remote deserts to crowded modern cities. Their many innate abilities allow them to survive under these diverse conditions. Central to their adaptability is their ability to hunt, which has not been affected by domestication.

Wherever your cat ends up living, it would spend all of its time in a fixed area referred to as its home range. The home range would be large enough to provide sufficient food or prey to sustain your cat. A home range contains, in addition to food left by humans, populations of insects, mice, birds and a variety of other prey, all of which would be fair game for your cat.

Your cat's primary living area, where it would spend most of its time, is on a smaller portion of its home range called its territory. Your cat would defend its territory fiercely from intrusion by strange cats.

The state of your cat's home range would be extremely important to it. It would take an intense interest in other cats and animals that are present. Your cat would roam about its home range frequently, using a network of paths, to keep tabs on it. As a result, it would be very familiar with the area, knowing where there are good places to climb, to hide, and to hunt. This familiarity would give your cat a sense of security.

Your cat would communicate with other animals by leaving scent marks in the form of urine, feces and glandular secretions. Scent marks allow cats to communicate with each other safely at a distance. Your cat would routinely check and refresh its marks and would be highly receptive to the scent messages left by other cats.

Would your cat live alone or in a group? Cats can live alone, or in groups that vary widely in both size and character. Whether or not your cat would end up living in a group or on its own depends on the amount and type of food sources in the area, the availability of shelter, your cat's gender, and, of course, its personality.

Your Cat At A Glance

If your cat were to find itself far from civilization, its only source of food would be the prey it caught. If this were the case, your cat would live a solitary life with the exception of mating or, if female, rearing its young. On the other hand, if your cat lived near humans, it could rely on both hunting and scavenging for food. It could find food in trash cans and garbage Dumpsters as well as food left out intentionally.

Living such a life, your cat would likely find itself in the company of numerous other cats. Life in groups, called colonies, is typical for cats living near humans. Cat colonies normally form around one or more (usually related) adult females, called queens, and their offspring. Adult male cats are not usually constant members of the group but do stay in the vicinity of the females. Males may split their time among several different colonies. Male kittens living in a colony eventually mature and usually leave or are driven from the group.

Though cats are often considered to be asocial, they do seek out the company of other cats. Your cat might form strong bonds with specific cats in its group. If your cat is female and unspayed it would have several litters of kittens every year, contributing to an increase in the local feral cat population.

In this life as an outdoor cat, your cat would spend its time scavenging and hunting, resting, roaming and interacting with other cats on its home range. This life, while free and natural for cats, would leave your cat susceptible to the many dangers posed by modern environments. Cars, dogs and other animals, cat fights in overcrowded city environments, and diseases, all contribute to a much shorter lifespan for outdoor cats than for their indoor counterparts. These are the very dangers that have helped give rise to the phenomenon of indoor cats, who, while being kept safe and healthy indoors, are deprived of the stimulation that an outdoor life provides.

Walk Your Cat

The life described above is meant to provide insight into how your cat sees the world and also tell the story of the modern domestic cat. But this story is not complete. By walking your cat, you are adding a new chapter to this story by helping to create a class of cats who enjoy the best of both worlds—indoor cats whose owners take them outdoors for walks.

To conclude your tour through the world of walking cats, we return to our feline bloggers, and imagine what would preoccupy their thoughts in a world where being walked is a normal part of life for indoor cats. No longer would "boredom" dominate discussions. Instead, feline bloggers would have turned their attention to all those things that naturally preoccupy cats. Articles sharing hunting tips with titles such as "Using the sound of passing cars as cover to sneak towards prey" would abound, while social gossip of the "goings on" in the home range would, to the disapproval of some, make up a sizable portion of discussions. A select group of sympathetic felines would reflect on the problems faced by feral cats, who do not benefit from the safety and comfort of indoor life. But overall, the tone would be optimistic. With typical feline satisfaction, some more philosophical commentators would reflect with pride on life with humans and on the new paradigm of the modern domestic cat.

REFERENCES

The authors found the following books particularly useful while writing this book:

Beaver, Bonnie V. 2003. *Feline Behavior: A Guide For Veterinarians*. 2nd ed. St. Louis, MO: Saunders.

Case, Linda P. 2003. *The Cat: Its Behavior, Nutrition, & Health.* Ames, Iowa: Iowa State Press.

Turner, Dennis, C. and Patrick Bateson, eds. 2000. *The Domestic Cat: The Biology Of Its Behaviour.* 2nd ed, Cambridge UK; New York: Cambridge University Press.

Walk Your Cat

Index

A

"act of nature," 71
activities, *see* outdoor activities
adaptability of species, 123-124
aggression, 48, 51, 63, 72, 107-108
    body language, 107-108
    dealing with, 72, 108
    reasons for, 108
    rewarding, 72
    territorial, 48-49
animals, encounters with, 36-38
arched back, 107
arguing, usefulness of, 67-68
associations, 19, 53, 55, 60, 77, 84, 93
    accidental, 19, 84
    positive, 68
    trained, 14
atmospheric temperature
    importance of, 110
attachment to places, 38
attention seeking skills, 15
avoidance of places, 61

B

bad experiences, 96, 98-99
basic needs, 123
behavioral modification
    techniques, 5, 13-25
body language, 29, 51, 91, 100-108
    aggression, 107
    approachable, 104

body language (continued)
    calm and relaxed, 103
    ears, *see* ears
    body profile
        exaggerating, 107
        lowering, 105
    fear, 105
    guidelines for reading, 103
    hunting, 104
    play, 29
    pupils, *see* eyes
    reliance on, 101
    tail, *see* tail
    uncertain, 105
body posture, 103, 104, 105, 106
body structure, 119
bond with owner, 12, 29, 90
boredom, 4
breed, effect on training, 6, 90
bridge-words, 21
    and classical conditioning, 21
broken associations, causes, 83-84

C

carrying cat indoors, 66, 68
    see also punishments
cat-human communication, 102
cat-human relationship, 48, 102, 123, 126
cat
    introductions, 48-51

cat (continued)
  societies, 27
    see also colonies
  relating to, 28
  proper handling on walks, 33
    see also leash handling
cat-walking principle, 32
  caveat to, 32
cautiousness, 89
chaperone, role as, 28
choking, 7, 81, 82
classical conditioning, 14-15
  downside to, 15
claws, 41-42, 45, 119
climbing, risks of, 116
  see also tree climbing
coercion, response to, 28
colonies, 125
communication, 100
communication at a distance
  see scent marks
concentration
  breaking, 76, 80
  telltale sign of break in, 76
confidence-building experiences, 60
conflict, 62-68
  avoiding, 52-53, 62, 66, 68
    by carrying indoors, 66, 68
  recognizing, 62
consistency, importance of, 18, 23-24, 64, 78, 83
control
  adjusting, 58
  cat testing limits of, 86
  importance of maintaining, 99

D

danger 37
  detecting, 14, 57
  escaping, see escaping danger
  see also safety

dead-weight maneuver, 65-66
defensive posture, 65
depression, 4
desensitization, 96-98
directing, 57, 70-78, 87, 88
  from a standstill, 73
  using the leash, 57-59, 70-78
  without pulling, 71
disapproval from owner
  response to, 29
discomfort, recognizing, 33, 110-111
disobedience, reasons for, 29, 79
dogs, 29, 35, 37, 49, 121
  trainability, 29
domestication, effects of, 31, 123
duration of walks, 66

E

ears, 103, 104, 106, 108, 121
  drawn back, reasons for, 106, 108
  watching during walks, 121
endurance, 44, 45, 119
environmental changes
  effect on walks, 90
equipment, 6-9
escaped cat, catching, 97
escaping danger, 44, 119
  preferred method of, 44
excessive enthusiasm, 6-7, 78, 81
  dealing with, 78
exposure, 51, 94, 96, 98
  need for, 94
exposure distance
  desensitization, 98
  habituation, 96
eyes, 106, 107, 120

F

familiarity, 38-39, 61, 87, 124
  benefits of, 61

Index

familiarity (continued)
    impact on pace of walking, 38
fear, 105-107
    gauging, 97
    spectrum of, 105
feline bloggers, 1, 126
feline perspective, 24, 101
    importance of, 101
felis catus, 2
fleas, 113, 114
food sources, 124-125
food treats, use of, 54
futility, 18-19, 23, 64, 65, 71-72, 83
    importance of consistency, 18

G

gait, 119
The Good, The Bad And The Ugly, 49
grass
    eating, 42-44
    walking on, 112
group living, conditions for, 124
guide, role as, 28

H

habituation, 94-96
    importance for kittens, 95
harness
    anxiety, 55-56
    associating with outdoors, 53-54
        guidelines for, 54
    backing out of, 63-64
    fit, 55, 63
    impractical, 7-8
    putting on, 10, 53-55
    recommended, 8
hearing, 121
    hunting by, 121
heartworms, 114
heatstroke, 110-111

hierarchy, absence of, 27
    see also cat societies
high places, 19, 24
home range, 40, 49, 124
hot surfaces, sitting on, 110
howling at door, 18
hunting, 13, 45, 104, 119, 121
    on a leash, 45-46
    skills, 13, 20, 126

I

indoor cats, 1-4, 33
indoor life, benefits of, 125
indoor routine, breaking, 33-34
infectious diseases, 114-115
insects, 113
intelligence vs. motivation
    influence on training, 26, 29

J

jumping on tables, 19, 23, 24

K

kittenhood, prolonged, 28

L

learning, types of, 20, 90
leash
    handling, 57-59
    pulling, 75, 76, 77
    recommended, 8-9
    safety, 115-117
    short, taut, 58
    slack, 58
local risks, 110
long grass, walking through, 73

M

maintainenance, 22, 81, 83,84-86, 93
   checklist for, 85
meowing, 15
   see also, cat-human communication
mobility, 110, 119
   importance for temperature regulation, 110
modern domestic cats, 2, 123-126
modern environments
   dangers posed by, 125
mosquitoes, 114
mother-kitten type relationship, 28
   see also, cat-human relationship
motivation, 26-34
   difficulty with cats, 27
   in leash-training, 30-31

N

natural activities, 3, 31-32
natural life, 31, 123-126
need for outdoors, 2-3, 31-32
nervousness, recognizing, 90-91
new environments, feeling out, 59
"No!", cats' response to, 83

O

operant conditioning, 15-22
outdoor activities, 39-47
outdoors, as motivator, 31-32
over-control, reasons to avoid, 73

P

pace of walks, 72, 87, 89
panic, avoiding, 92
paths, walking on, 61
Pavlov, 15

personal space, 36, 50, 51, 87, 108
personality, influence on walking, 90
poisons, 112-113
predictability, importance of, 58-59
pressure, sense of touch, 122
prey, risks of eating, 115
punishments, 16-18, 66, 68
   indirect vs. direct, 17
   problems with, 17
   recommended for cats, 17
   used in leash-training, 17
   when to use, 18, 68

R

rain, walking in, 47
reassurance, 28-30, 89-99
   limitations of, 92-93
   techniques, 91-93
   vocal, 91-92, 93, 97
refusal behaviors, 53, 62-63
replacement, 19
resting, 46, 67, 77
   on walks, 46
   vocal cue for, 82
restraining cats, 33, 53
retraining, 84, 86
   broken associations, 84
returning indoors, 62, 66-68
   tips for, 66-68
rewards 16-18, 21, 22
   delay in giving, 21
   effective types, 16
   proper usage, 16
   schedule for giving, 16, 22
rotating, 76-77,82
routine, 24, 33-34, 66, 98
   duration of walks, 66
   in training, 24
   see also predictability

Index

S

safety, 37, 88, 115-117
  on leash, 37
scent
  communication, 41, 124
  marks, 40-41
scratching, 19, 41-42
self-reliance, 27
sense stimulation, 3
senses, 101, 119-123
sensitization, 14-15, 98
  see also desensitization
shade, need for, 111
shaping, 21-22, 84
side cover, 73
signs of poisoning, *see* poisons
slowing down, 81, 87
small apartments, 4
smell, 40, 121-122
snow, walking in, 47
stalling, preventing, 67
standing position, 56, 75
start walking, training cats to, 76, 80
stings, 113
sociability, 48, 125
social behavior, 27, 36, 121-122, 124
  compared to human, 27
social distance, 36-38
  comfortable, 37
socialization
  importance of for kittens, 49, 95
solitary living, conditions for, 125
sores, 111
stopping, 81, 87, 97
  a frightened cat, 63, 97
stress, 33
stroking lower back, 92, 93
submissiveness, 27, 29
sunburn, 111
sunscreen, 111

T

tail, 104, 105, 107
  arch at base of, 107
talking to cats, effect of, 91-92
temperature
  sense of touch, 122
  toleration, 110
  see also heatstroke
territorial behavior, 49
territory, 40, 49, 124
ticks, 113
time-out, 66
timing, 19-20
touch, 122-123
training
  forgetting, 22
  duration of, 5-6
  importance of communication, 23
  importance of motivation, 26
  methods, 13-25
  most effective methods, 23
  role of owner, 27
traumatic incidents, 14-15, 98
tree climbing, 44-45, 119
  risks, 45, 116
trial and error learning, 20, 72
tuggling, 74-75

U

unfamiliar "creatures," 38

V

vaccinations, 114
venturing outdoors, 59-61
vision
  color, importance of, 120
  detail 92
  field of, 56
  movement, 120

visual recognition, 92
vocal cues, 67, 79-84, 87, 93
   appropriate types, 80
   inadvertent associations, 83
   useful examples, 80-84
      "Inside," 83
      "It's okay," 93
      "Let's go," 80
      "No," 83
      "Outside," 79, 83, 84
      "Slow down", 81
      "Stop", 81
      "Turn back", 82
      "Wait", 82
vomeronasal organ, 121

W

wait, training cats to, 77, 82
walking
   benefits of, 4
   duration of, 59-60, 66
   locations, 35-38
      guidelines for, 37-38
      expanding, 61
   preferred times, 47
   two cats, 81, 86-88
      tips for, 87-88
whiskers, 103, 106, 122
whistling, 80
wild catnip, 44